Jacob's Ladder

NEW QUILTS from an OLD FAVORITE

edited by
Linda Baxter Lasco

American Quilter's Society

P.O. Box 3290 • Paducah, KY 42002-3290
Fax 270-898-1173 • e-mail: orders@AQSquilt.com

PATHWAYS, detail. Full quilt on page 54.

Thank You Sponsors

JANOME

moda

Located in Paducah, Kentucky, the American Quilter's Society (AQS) is dedicated to promoting the accomplishments of today's quilters. Through its publications and events, AQS strives to honor today's quiltmakers and their work and to inspire future creativity and innovation in quiltmaking.

Executive Book Editor: Andi Milam Reynolds
Senior Editor: Linda Baxter Lasco
Graphic Design: Lynda Smith
Cover Design: Michael Buckingham
Quilt Photography: Charles R. Lynch
Museum Photography: Susan Edwards

©2013, American Quilter's Society

Library of Congress Cataloging-in-Publication Data

Jacob's ladder : new quilts from an old favorite / edited by Linda Baxter Lasco.

    pages cm
  Summary: "With the traditional Jacob's Ladder block as a starting point, a variety of original interpretations are showcased in the "New Quilts from an Old Favorite" contest from The National Quilt Museum. Quilts selected for their excellence in design, technique, and innovation show how differently the selected traditional pattern can be interpreted"--Provided by publisher.
  ISBN 978-1-60460-062-9
  1. Quilts. 2. Jacob's ladder (Biblical dream) in art. 3. Quilting--Competitions--United States. I. Lasco, Linda Baxter.
  TT835.J32 2013
  746.46--dc23

                    2013002158

Additional copies of this book may be ordered from the American Quilter's Society, PO Box 3290, Paducah, KY 42002-3290, or online at www.AmericanQuilter.com.

Cover Quilt: First-place winner, GREEN WITH ENVY, A TRIBUTE TO WOMEN IN FABRIC, made by Peggy Fetterhoff, Spring, Texas

Title Page: Third-place winner, UPSTAIRS, DOWNSTAIRS, made by Timna Tarr, South Hadley, Massachusetts

Proudly printed and bound in the
United States of America

Dedication

This book is dedicated to all those who see a traditional quilt as both a link to the past and a bridge to the future.

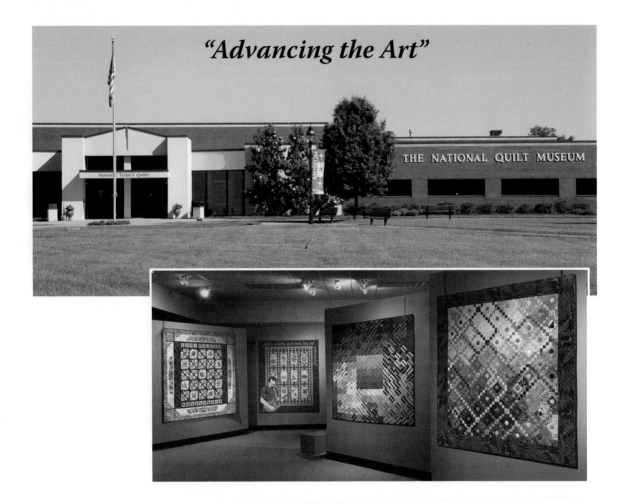

"Advancing the Art"

This book is dedicated to all those who see a traditional quilt and visualize both its link to the past and its bridge to the future.

The National Quilt Museum is an exciting place where the public can learn about quilts, quiltmaking, quiltmakers, and experience quilts that inspire and delight.

Annually visited by quilters and art enthusiasts worldwide, the Museum aims to advance the art of quilting by bringing quilt and fiber art to new and expanding audiences around the world.

Contents

Preface

While preservation of the past is one of The National Quilt Museum's core functions, one of its greatest services is performed as it links the past to the present and to the future. With that goal in mind, The National Quilt Museum sponsors an annual contest and exhibit—New Quilts from an Old Favorite (NQOF).

Created both to acknowledge our quiltmaking heritage and to recognize innovation, creativity, and excellence, the contest challenges today's quiltmakers to interpret a single traditional quilt block in a new and exciting work of their own design. Each year contestants respond with a myriad of stunning interpretations.

Jacob's Ladder: New Quilts from an Old Favorite is a collection of these interpretations. In this book, you'll find a brief description of the 2013 contest, followed by the five award winners and fifteen additional finalists and their quilts.

Full-color photographs of the quilts accompany each quiltmaker's comments—comments that provide insight into their widely diverse creative processes. The winners' and finalists' tips, techniques, and patterns offer an artistic framework for your own interpretation. In addition, information about The National Quilt Museum is included.

Our wish is that *Jacob's Ladder: New Quilts from an Old Favorite* will further our quiltmaking heritage as new quilts based on these block are inspired by the outstanding quilts contained within.

Left and opposite: JL Tribute, detail. Full quilt on page 72.

The Contest

One of the roles of a museum is not only to preserve the past, but also to link the past to the present and to the future. With that knowledge at heart, The National Quilt Museum holds New Quilts from an Old Favorite, an annual contest and exhibit. Created to acknowledge our quiltmaking heritage and to recognize innovation, creativity, and excellence, the contest challenges today's quiltmakers to interpret a single traditional quilt block in a work of their own design.

The contest requires that quilts entered be recognizable in some way as a variation on that year's selected traditional block. The quilts must be no larger than 80" and no smaller than 50" on a side. Each quilt entered must be quilted. Quilts may only be entered by the maker(s) and must have been completed after December 31 two years prior to the entry date.

Quiltmakers are asked to send in two images—one of the full quilt and one detail—for jurying. Three jurors view these and consider technique, artistry, and interpretation of the theme block to select 18 finalists. These finalist quilts are then sent to the Museum where a panel of three judges carefully evaluates them. This evaluation of the actual quilts focuses on design, innovation, theme, and workmanship. The first- through fifth-place winners are then selected and notified.

An exhibit of the 18 quilts opens at The National Quilt Museum in Paducah, Kentucky, each spring, and then travels to venues around the country for two years. Thousands of quilt lovers have enjoyed these exhibits at their local or regional museum.

A book is produced by the American Quilter's Society featuring full-color photos of the finalists and award-winning quilts; biographical information about each quilter; and their tips and techniques. The book provides an inside look at how quilts are created and a glimpse into the artistic mindset of today's quilters.

Previous theme blocks have been Double Wedding Ring, Log Cabin, Kaleidoscope, Mariner's Compass, Ohio Star, Pineapple, Storm at Sea, Bear's Paw, Tumbling Blocks, Feathered Star, Monkey Wrench, Seven Sisters, Dresden Plate, Sawtooth, Sunflower, Orange Peel, and Baskets. The block selected for 2013 is Jacob's Ladder. Carolina Lily and Nine-Patch will be the feature blocks for 2014 and 2015, respectively.

NQM would like to thank this year's New Quilts from an Old Favorite contest sponsors: MODA Fabrics and Janome America, Incorporated.

Above: BLIZZARD, detail. Full quilt on page 24.

The Jacob's Ladder Block

One aspect of the Jacob's Ladder block stands out: it is created from squares and triangles. In its simplest form, it is a Four-Patch block made up of four-patch units and half-square triangles. This version was published under the name Grandmother Clark in 1932[1]. If you grow the block a bit, it becomes a Nine-Patch made of the same units. This version is earlier, found in Marie Webster's book *Quilts: Their Story and How to Make Them*, published in 1915[2]. A diamond One-Patch pattern was published under the name Jacob's Ladder in *Woman's Day* magazine in the 1940s and in *This Week* in 1953[3]. A third version made of Flying Geese units was published by Grandma Dexter in the 1930s[4]. This all points to how the Jacob's Ladder pattern was part of the marketing explosion when quilting became popular in the period after World War I.

If one considers only the versions made of four-patch units and half-square triangles, there are 127 Jacob's Ladder quilts listed in the *Quilt Index*[5] from 1840 to the present.

The largest number of Jacob's Ladder quilts was made from 1890 to 1920. This was also the time of very simple cotton fabrics. Monochromatic prints in navy, red, cadet blue, claret, and black were the palette of the day, with polychromatic "neon" colors over black also found. Shirtings were the light ground fabrics. The overall quality of the fabric was not good; the cotton cloth was thin and didn't last well.[6]

The first half of this period found the United States taking its place as the major manufacturing force in the world. Between 1865 and 1910, railroads increased track miles eightfold. Prosperity came to the middle class, and women could buy ready-made clothing for themselves and their families. Quilting fell out of favor. Cotton quilts were deemed old-fashioned. The decline of hand-sewing skills and complexity of technique and construction in cotton quilts was becoming evident.[7] When the Crazy Quilt came on the scene in the 1880s, fancy needlework was taken up as an expression of artistic accomplishment and leisure; such quilts were not meant for beds.

The large number of Jacob's Ladder quilts made between 1890 and 1920 reflects all these influences. After the sea change in cloth quality, palette, and print style, when the bright pastels of the 1920s came on the market, quilting became popular again. The Jacob's Ladder pattern continued to be made in these refreshing colors. Based on the *Quilt Index* analysis, the period from 1925 to 1949 saw the second-most quantities of Jacob's Ladder quilts made.

Sometimes simple things stand the test of time. The Jacob's Ladder quilt block is one of these things. When quilting was in decline after the Civil War and later during the Crazy Quilt fad, quilts of the Jacob's Ladder pattern continued to be made, pulling this most basic of quilt block constructions through to today. Now we can enjoy the Jacob's Ladder quilts of the past while tapping this pattern to create some of the most innovative quilts of today.

Judy Schwender
Curator of Collections/Registrar
The National Quilt Museum

1   Barbara Brackman, *Encyclopedia of Pieced Quilt Patterns*; American Quilter's Society: Paducah, Kentucky, 1993; 176-177, 522.
2   Ibid, 215, 527.
3   Ibid, 26-27, 527.
4   Ibid, 246-247, 522.
5   Found at http://www.quiltindex.org; accessed January 8, 2013 by the author.
6   Eileen Jahnke Trestain, *Dating Fabrics: A Color Guide 1800-1960*; American Quilter's Society: Paducah, Kentucky, 1998; 99.
7   Roderick Kiracofe, *The American Quilt: A History of Cloth and Comfort 1750-1950*; Clarkson Potter: New York; 1993; 139-178.

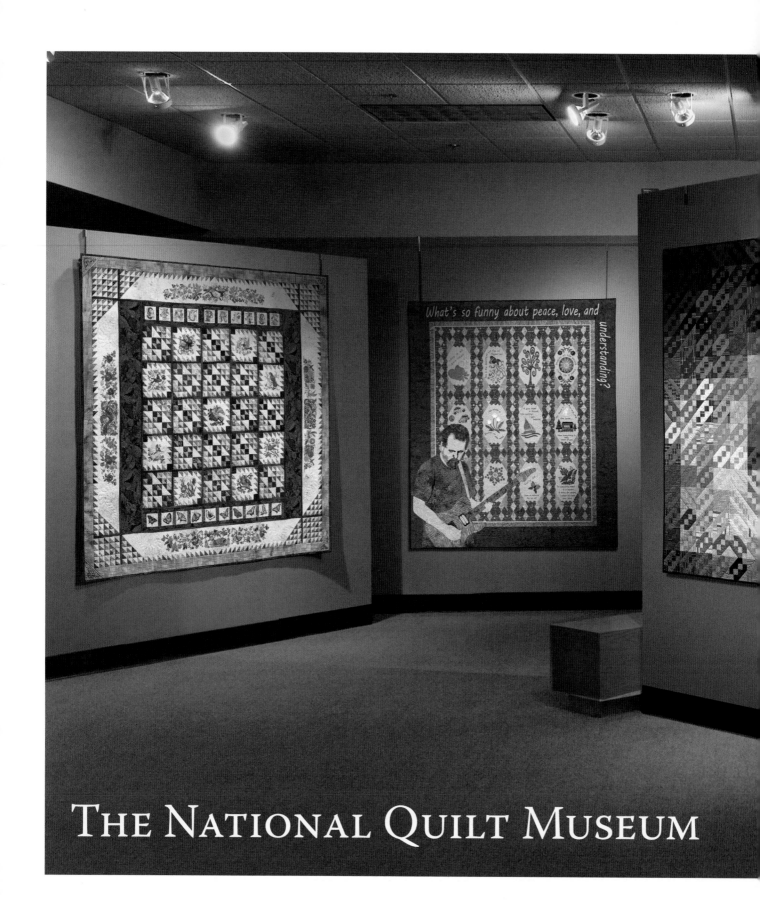

Inside the image: *What's so funny about peace, love, and understanding?*

THE NATIONAL QUILT MUSEUM

The National Quilt Museum
215 Jefferson Street • Paducah, Kentucky 42001
www.NationalQuiltMuseum.org • (270) 442-8856

Green With Envy:
A Tribute to Women in Fabric
55" x 55"

Photo by John DeFranco

First Place
Peggy Fetterhoff
Spring, Texas

Meet Peggy

I was born in Pennsylvania but grew up in Niagara Falls, New York. I moved to Houston, Texas, in 1974 where I raised my four children. I put myself through college while they were growing up, earning a degree in finance with a minor in computer science from the University of Houston. I retired from a chemical company in 2009 as a Senior IT Network Analyst. My family has grown to include five grandchildren and two great-grandchildren.

I have sewn since I was 12 years old, mainly focused on clothing and home décor items. After my four children left home, I experienced the empty nest syndrome that resulted in my finding new and interesting ways to enrich my life. In 1995 the discovery of quilting was part of that enrichment. This is the second time I've been a finalist in the New Quilts from an Old Favorite contest.

Quilting not only allowed me to become an artist but also provided me with a social life with a fascinating and diverse group of women. Early on I started collections of various images on fabric, one of which was on the subject of how women were depicted in fabric. One of the quilts I made for my three sons included one for my youngest single son with several pinup images of women. At first it seemed this was the dominating female image I found in fabric, which was not my favorite. With time, I have found many other types of female images, all of which have been added to my extensive collection.

One of my favorites is the image of the Indian woman who is at the top of the center of GREEN WITH ENVY.

This fabric has the most beautiful shades of pink and turquoise over a brown/beige background. I have searched for other fabrics similar to it but have never found anything close. I also love the contrast between the image of the traditional costume of the Indian woman and the very contemporary garment of the woman on the bottom center.

The first quilt I completed in this series on women in fabric was a collage from my collection for my granddaughter, Briana. I liked this quilt so much that I also completed one for myself using a different color scheme. My pleasure in this collection continues as I find more female images in fabric that lead to new unique design ideas.

The inspiration for my art is a reflection of the way I view the world. I visualize color everywhere in curving perspectives. Fabric is my paint! I have always loved art but did not realize I had any artistic talent until I discovered colorwash or watercolor quilts. These techniques have been influential in the way I create fiber art.

My pieces have many of the elements and characteristics of impressionist paintings. By combining hundreds to thousands of different fabrics with varied patterns and colors, I am able to create unique original designs. The fabric pieces can take on any size and shape from squares to hexagons that allow the designs to flow in multiple directions. The final fiber art creation originates from this innovative process.

Inspiration and Design

The inspiration for all my designs is driven by the fabric itself as fabric is my paint. I prefer commercial fabric to making my own because there is such a large variety to choose from to stimulate my imagination. GREEN WITH ENVY: A TRIBUTE TO WOMEN IN FABRIC comes from my fabric collection that was assembled over several years. All of the female images were printed on fabric by textile manufacturers. The feminine themes include a diversity of different ethnic groups, pinups, angels, and mermaids. Some are humorous and some contain historical images from various periods in history.

Although I do not normally work from established patterns or blocks, I often use them as a starting point for a design. My previous experience with the Jacob's Ladder block was working with a group of women on a quilt for our Woodlands Quilt Guild auction.

I have a large studio on the second floor of my house that was custom-built by my youngest son and my brother. It includes three different size fleece-covered walls that I use to create my original designs. The fabric sticks to the fleece on the walls, which pro-

vides flexibility to move pieces without using pins. All of my creations begin by moving fabric pieces around on these walls until a design starts to form.

First I decide on a color theme for the piece. Then I sort through my extensive fabric collection for the chosen colors. I generally only purchase fabrics in one-third yard sizes resulting in a very large stash of small pieces of fabric. Once I have started on a design, I also start shopping for new fabric to expand on the palette that I am working on. I carry around snippets of fabric sewn on a muslin background to make sure I don't stray too far from the original color scheme.

Technique

The Jacob's Ladder pattern has a lot of blocks with half-square triangles. I used the method of drawing lines on the back of fabric squares, sewing ¼" on each side of the lines, and then cutting the blocks apart, pressing, and trimming for accuracy. This prevents the problem of sewing on bias and distorting the squares. To provide an extensive palette to work from on the design walls, I use hundreds of different fabrics for cutting and sewing multiple pieces in the chosen color scheme.

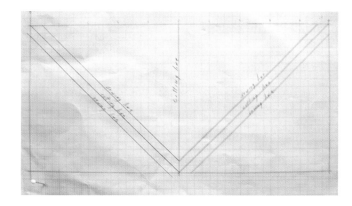

With this particular piece, I began by using pink colors on a black background. (It is still on my design wall only partially sewn.) It wasn't until I completed the design on the wall that I realized that the pink

"To provide an extensive palette to work from, I use hundreds of different fabrics for cutting and sewing multiple pieces in the chosen color scheme."

did not stand out enough against the black-and-white background. The second problem was I used 2" squares, which did not provide enough viewing space for the female images. GREEN WITH ENVY is the second attempt using the same design but larger 3" blocks for better viewing of the female images.

The original concept was to place the female images in the center of each block, then weave the green lines in and around the black-and-white background.

While working on the design wall, I also attempted to use drawings on the computer but could not get the design in the interior of the piece to come together. What I discovered on the design wall was that in order to merge the center of this concept the side V's needed to be one block larger than the top and bottom V's. Once all the green lines came together, the center had more space to focus on larger images.

All of the fabric in this piece is shaded from light on the top to dark on the bottom to provide more dimension to the design. To complete the quilt, one more component was included by adding a small quarter-square at each end of the green stripe in the pieced border. This suggests the illusion of the green stripes floating on the dark background.

understanding?

Peace, Love & Rock 'n Roll
57" x 66"

Photo by Don Watts

Second Place
Karen Watts
Mayhill, New Mexico

Meet Karen

I've been a quilter for 21 years now, and have never grown tired of it. There are always new techniques to try, beautiful new fabric to use, and different fibers to experiment with. After using only cotton for many years, I've been having fun with silk and wool as well. I'm also experimenting with more abstract designs. Going to quilt shows, designing challenge quilts, and having quilting retreats with friends are some of my favorite pastimes and sources of inspiration.

This has been a great year in my quilting life. When I first started quilting, I had to use the kitchen table (in a tiny house in Southern California), then moved to Houston and used the smallest bedroom, later expanded to two rooms, and in May of 2012 I was able to move into my own studio! We moved permanently to our vacation home in the mountains of New Mexico in 2011, and there was really no good place to sew. Since there were seven acres available, we built a separate studio, complete with deck, fire pit, and hot tub.

The sewing area includes a design wall.

Fabric storage includes cutting and ironing areas; the bathroom is the open door on the left. The wood door leads to the mechanical room, and the entrance with mud room is to the right.

It's been so nice to have everything out of boxes and in one place; I hardly know what I want to work on next. And I've been easily distracted by the view from my windows. We have a lot of wildlife around us: deer, elk, and even bears! One day I was working on my contest quilt and looked up to see a curious little buck looking in my window.

I know I am incredibly lucky to have such a beautiful place to work, but my husband tells me building a quilt studio was in *his* best interests, too! He had his eye on the study in the house to use as a recording studio and was concerned that might be the only option for a sewing room. As you can see from my quilt, my husband is a guitar player, and now the study is full of guitars, amps, microphones, a keyboard—you name it. He's been recording some of his friends and wants to start on his own album. Life is good.

Inspiration and Design

I always begin my designs in Electric Quilt® 7 (www. electricquilt.com) by either importing or drawing the basic block and then just playing around with it. I'll try it on point, straight set, combined with other blocks, with changes to the shape, etc. If something strikes me, I'll pursue it further. In this case, I noticed that setting the block on point could make an interesting sashing when used with alternate blocks. But instead of using the traditional square block I elongated it to a diamond, which I felt was more visually interesting.

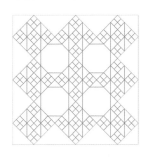
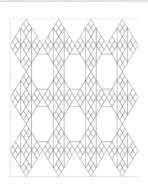

I needed a theme. What was my quilt about? While listening to music one day I got to thinking about songs that had a message. As I was growing up in the late '60s to early '70s many of the popular songs had a big impact on me, and I truly believed that a better world was possible. With all the turmoil still in the world, I felt that the lyrics of some of my favorite songs and the ideas behind them were just as important for people to hear today. I chose quotes from several songs, and designed appliqué to go with them.

I wanted the quilt to be colorful, but hadn't decided on colors yet. While browsing on www.equilter.com I found the blue fabric printed with peace, love, and joy. It was perfect!

I went back to the Jacob's Ladder block to see if I could give it a more '60s look. I accomplished this by changing the straight lines of the half-square triangles (now diamonds) to wavy lines. Of course that change did not allow me to piece that unit, so I used machine appliqué with a buttonhole stitch. I also added the wavy line corners on the alternate blocks to continue the sashing look.

"Going to quilt shows, designing challenge quilts, and having quilting retreats with friends are some of my favorite pastimes and sources of inspiration."

After deciding to use favorite song lyrics in the alternate blocks I got the idea to put my husband, Don, on the quilt. Don has been a guitar player for 45 years, played in countless bands, and his music has run the gamut from rock 'n roll, country rock, acoustic rock, finger-style, folk, and blues. I had taken a nice photo of him playing guitar the previous summer, and thought he'd be a great addition to my quilt. I had never tried anything like that before, so it was doubly appealing, just to see if I could pull it off. And I think he's pretty happy that I wanted to put him on my quilt!

Technique

I used Adobe® Photoshop® Elements to manipulate my photo, and mostly it was trial and error. The first step in interpreting my photo was to use a filter called poster edge. This sharply defined the areas of color and made it easier to see how I could simplify it to use fabric. I also made it a bit lighter. Then I turned it black and white.

Eliminating color makes it easier to see different areas of value, and also doesn't distract you with reality. As you can see, I exercised my artistic license and changed all the color—Don has never had red hair, his shirt was gray, and his guitar, blonde. Next I determined how large I wanted the figure and printed it out full-size, using many sheets of paper and taping them together.

I used a Sharpie® marker to outline the areas that would use a different fabric, simplifying as I went. For example, Don's shirt was one piece of fabric, with some dark pieces added for the folds under his arm. I wanted the quilt to look like him, but I wasn't aiming for a totally realistic portrait.

With my areas outlined, I turned my enlarged printout over and traced the shapes onto fusible web. This reversed the shapes, as the web is then ironed to the wrong side of the chosen fabric. With all the shapes cut out I started building the image separate from the quilt top, buttonhole stitching the pieces as I went. I didn't add the figure to the quilt top until it was all together in one piece, then I only needed to do the last buttonhole stitching around the perimeter. I used Sulky® rayon thread for the buttonhole stitching, matching the thread color to the fabric.

Upstairs Downstairs
52½" x 66¾"

Photo by Suzanne Lea Larocque

Third Place
Timna Tarr
South Hadley, Massachusetts

Meet Timna

I come from a long line of quilters. My dad has quilts that were made for him by his great-grandma and great-grandpa. Grandpa cut out the pieces while Grandma sewed them together. While I was growing up, my mom and maternal grandma always had quilts in progress. They each made their own quilts, but sometimes Grandma would make a top and Mom would do the quilting for her. When the hand-quilting frame was up at Grandma's house, whoever was visiting could stitch on the quilt. It didn't matter how young you were or how big you made your stitches, she was happy to have you contribute.

My mother taught me to use her sewing machine when I was about seven years old, but I did not enjoy sewing at all while I was living at home. Quilts were pretty boring, too!

Fifteen years ago, shortly after I graduated from college with a degree in art history, I made my first quilt. Not wanting to let on to my family that I might be interested in quilting, I borrowed a sewing machine and made the top in secret. Since I did not know that I could learn to quilt from a book or by taking a class, I made it up on my own, remembering bits and pieces of how Mom quilted. I used cardboard templates and my measuring left a lot to be desired—what were supposed to be diamonds actually turned out to be octagons. Even though that first quilt is quite ugly and has many "issues," I immediately loved the challenge of quilting. Over the next few years I machine pieced and hand quilted several quilts, obsessively.

In 2001, with a loan from my mom, I bought a long-arm machine and started quilting for other people. It was the best training in quiltmaking I could ask for as many of my clients are accomplished quilters. Working on their quilts and looking at the backs of their quilt tops has been a master class in the technical aspects of quilting. I learned things like the importance of pressing direction, trimming seam allowances, avoiding the shadowing of fabrics, and how to match thread color by on-the-job-training. Seeing so many different styles of quilts also taught me a tremendous amount about color and pattern.

Currently I spend about 20 percent of my working life quilting for other people and the rest of my time making quilts for show and sale. This balance is working for my family right now, as it allows me time to be creative and to be home with my seven-year-old daughter when necessary.

Inspiration

I was encouraged to enter the NQOF challenge by my Round Robin member and fellow contestant Ann Feitelson. Ann and I often share our works-in-progress, and encourage each other in our quilting lives. The spring before the entry deadline, I told Ann that there was no way I would enter because I did not like the Jacob's Ladder block. Well, I'm good at saying, "I will never..." and then doing it. I might not have liked the block, but I do like a challenge. My goal was to use the block to create a quilt I liked and was proud of. After spending many hours with Jacob's Ladder, I still cannot say that it is my favorite block, but I have a new respect for it.

Much of my work incorporates appliquéd circles. When I do not have a large project in the works, I hand appliqué circles on squares to keep my hands busy. There are often stacks of appliquéd blocks in my studio waiting for a project. While thinking about the contest, I made several traditional Jacob's Ladder blocks using 1" squares for the ladders. When those blocks were on my design wall, I realized my current pile of circle blocks fit between the ladders perfectly. With that discovery, UPSTAIRS DOWNSTAIRS was born.

I knew I would see this quilt through to the end—and would probably like it! Since the circle blocks were already made, I constructed the ladder blocks, pairing up colors I liked. After making as many ladders as I could tolerate, I arranged them on the design wall. It was only then that I added in the circle blocks and sewed the top together.

At this point in the game I was quite pleased with myself. I had the top finished! That is until I measured the quilt. It was not big enough to fit the entry requirements. I was happy with the top as it was, and afraid if I added more piecing I would detract from the composition rather than add to it. But I was confident that I could add a border and use quilting to enhance the pieced work, so I went shopping for border fabric.

After auditioning many fabrics, I bought the perfect border fabric (and a few "backup" pieces, just in case) at my local quilt shop only to return home and realize that none of the fabrics worked at all. The border fabric I ended up using was in my stash the whole time, and the newly purchased "perfect" piece is now on the back of the quilt. Luckily, my measuring mistake was a very happy accident. The border frames the

pieced work and the quilt is more cohesive with the border than it was without it.

I decided to use quilting designs that I love and are representative of my quilting. My favorite motif to quilt is spirals, so I quilted little fiddlehead spirals in the backgrounds behind the ladders. I stitched in the ditch around the ladders to bring them into the foreground. Since I wanted the circles to pop, but did not want a prominent stitching line, I hand quilted around them. As for the border, I knew its quilting needed to tie all of the elements together. I did this by quilting lines on a 45-degree diagonal, ½" apart, to emphasize the direction of the ladders. The little circles quilted in every other channel reference back to the appliquéd circles. I used Quilters Dream 100-percent wool batting because I like how it creates dimension within a quilt. Where the quilting is heavy, the batting flattens out, and where there is little quilting the batting puffs up and literally gives the quilt an added depth.

Technique

My technique for laying out color is all about making a smooth background palette. I make each quilt block as its own small composition, picking two fabrics that I like together and sewing them into the block. In the block construction phase, I am only concerned with the paired fabrics and how they look together, rarely thinking about how each block is going to work with the rest of the quilt.

One thing I am aware of as I make blocks is that I need to have a variety of light, medium, and dark valued fabrics. The variety of values is what gives the quilt its sparkle. One other thing I do not pay attention to is the print on the fabric. I only care about what the color and value look like when I stand about 15 feet away from the fabric. UPSTAIRS DOWNSTAIRS has prints with houses, skulls and crossbones, and crowns. From a distance, one sees color and misses

> " *Much of my work incorporates appliquéd circles. When I do not have a large project in the works, I hand appliqué circles on squares to keep my hands busy.*"

many of the details, but it makes me giggle knowing they are in there.

Upstairs Downstairs has two different blocks, each having a foreground and a background. The first block is a circle (foreground) appliquéd on a square (background).

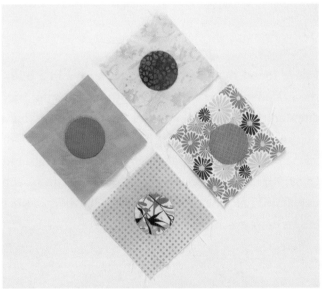

The second block is the ladder block that includes 1" squares that move diagonally through the quilt (foreground).

Once all of the blocks were made, I sorted the ladder blocks into piles based on their background color. Using only the backgrounds as a guide, I arranged the ladder blocks on my design wall, coaxing the color to flow from block to block. While arranging the blocks, I ignored the foreground color entirely.

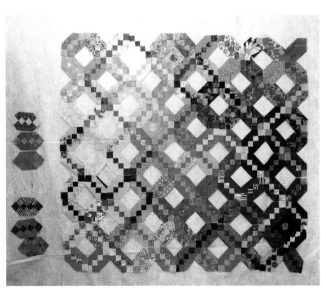

Sometimes I put contrasting colors next to each other to create a visual surprise. After the ladder blocks were arranged in a pleasing manner, I added in the circle blocks. Again, only looking at the background color, I placed the circle blocks in between the ladder blocks, looking for a smooth color transition from background to background.

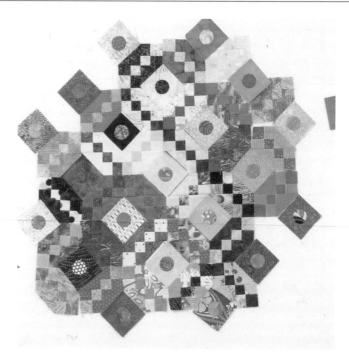

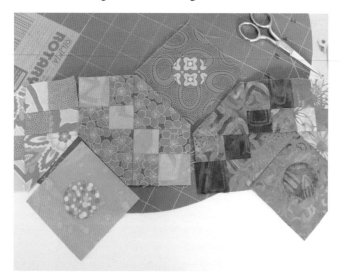

I have found that the more fabrics I have in a quilt, the easier it is to create a smooth background palette and the happier I am with the finished product. Because I only look at the background colors when laying out the blocks, the placement of the foreground colors turns out to be somewhat random. I think the unplanned placement of the foreground colors is what moves one's eye and gives the quilt interest.

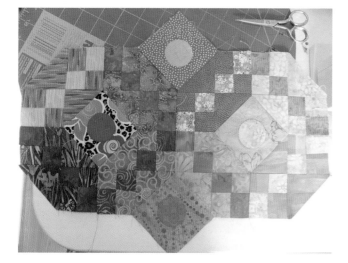

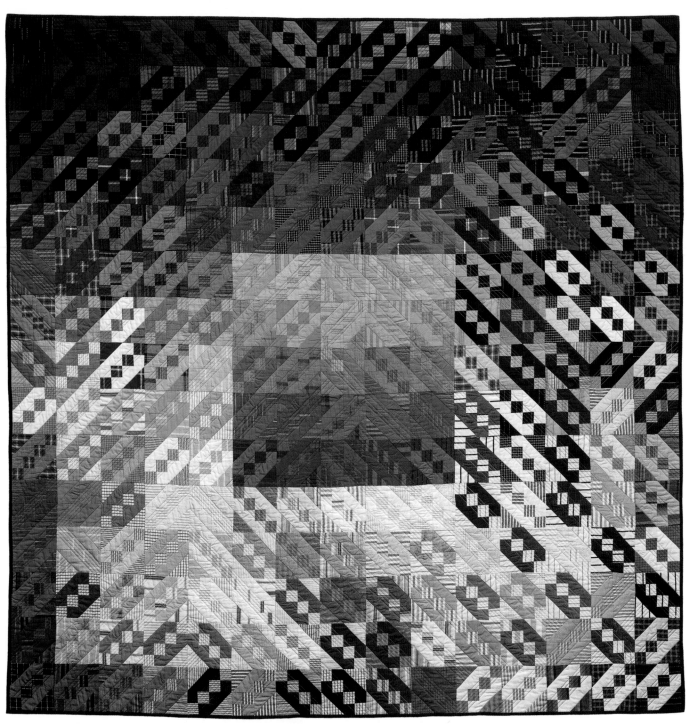

Blizzard
60" x 60"

Photo by Rachael Waring Fayroian

Fourth Place
Ann Feitelson
Montague, Massachusetts

Meet Ann

Two sources fuel my passion for quiltmaking. First, there's my mother. (Don't mothers always come first?) She adored color, pattern, and needlework, and because she did, I did. We avidly sewed, knit, and did needlepoint together. I often hear a quiet whisper from her, *"glorious,"* when I see a beautiful fabric or a striking color combination. She has been dead for five years, but I still hear it.

I would bet that my mother's delight in fiber and creativity came from *her* mother. Unfortunately, I didn't know my grandmother, whose name I share. She died while my mother was pregnant with me, but I have proof of her love of needlework: baby booties she knit for me, hats and purses she crocheted, and a sampler she stitched when she was only nine, which

has hung, always, in my parents' house and now in mine. It's as familiar to me as my palm, a guiding star for my own perseverance and desire to make beautiful things.

The other source I draw on is my art background. I was a college art major, and afterwards went to art school in New York City. I have an MFA in painting and an MA in Art History. I taught art; I write about art for local newspapers. I have been profoundly affected by the art-

ists whose work I studied and still love, by the work of my friends who were art students with me, by the aims of our teachers that we make something deeply personal, true to the moment, complex enough to embrace at least a few contradictions—*and* ravishing to the eye.

What sustains me here and now is my Round Robin. We are a group of 12 quilters who meet at each other's houses monthly and share projects in a variety of ways. A few people have come and gone, but this core of friends has remained consistent for a dozen years. Of course we have show and tell at each meeting, so I know the work of these people quite well—and they know mine. We appreciate each other; we check in with each other about exciting new quilt projects, and cheer each other on. For three years running I collaborated on a quilt for the New Quilts from an Old Favorite contest with one Round Robin member, Ronna Erickson. I'm pleased that another member, Timna Tarr, is one of this year's winners (page 19).

A haunting, disturbing question underlies this quilt. We had a massive blizzard in October 2011. It was an unusual time of year for a snowstorm; the trees were still in leaf. Wet, heavy snow was piling up rapidly; trees shattered under the weight—you could hear them snapping. Ten leggy grey birches had been planted along our driveway a few years before. The accumulating snow bent them over alarmingly, their top branches nearly touching the ground.

Several times during the night I went outside to shake the snow off the trees, hoping to save them.

When the trees sprang up, snow dumped down my collar, onto my face, and into my eyes. This was no snow-angel moment: something in me went wild as I shook the trees, countering the energy of the storm with my energy. They did survive (maybe I helped), and they did straighten up in the following days, but the questions won't let go of me: what would I do in a *real* emergency? These were, after all, just trees. How would you know if what you were doing was the *right* thing when you panicked, when there was no time, and few options? Did I save my trees? Could I save someone's life? Could I save my own?

I don't know. But I made a quilt about it. It is a dark quilt.

I wanted to create a snowed-in, multilayered, wind-blown dazzle. Black and white stripes, checks, and plaids would express snowiness. The visual overload of tiny graphic patterns would pile up like an infinity of snowflakes. And, like snowflakes, there would be no two blocks alike. The diagonals of the Jacob's Ladder blocks would represent falling, blowing snow.

I began making stark black-and-white-and-grey blocks, with a few flashes of color. I often start by making blocks in sets of 25, using five solids and five patterned fabrics, combining each with each, to make groups of interrelated colors.

Then I intersperse these groups with other groups.

The blacks and whites and the jagged shapes of my first several groups were initially pleasing, but in combination they were jarring, with overwhelming contrast.

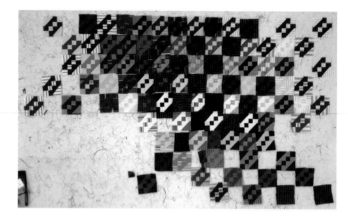

I tamed this discordant incoherence by organizing the quilt into a simple H-block (or Nine-Patch) division, with vibrant colors in the center, darkness above, and accumulating snow below. I enjoyed thinking about what colors would have the bright coldness of snow, which colors could create the visual shimmer of darkness. I realized, long after getting the idea to make a bright center square, that it was a kind of self-portrait.

Maybe because of the difficult questions the quilt represented, or because of its minimalist design, I had trouble bringing it to a conclusion. I thought I was pleased with areas where I'd somewhat randomly placed blocks; thought I was pleased with the multiple diagonals; thought the dull colors fit the subject; and began assembling blocks. At the end of the summer, I

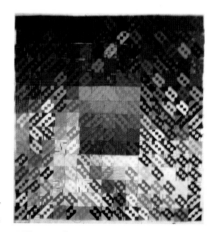

Ready to assemble (or so I thought).

"I am notorious in my Round Robin for agonizing and changing my mind, for revising almost-completed quilts, for ripping things that are begging to be finished. Just ask them!"

went away for two weeks to the Fine Arts Work Center in Provincetown, Massachusetts, with the quilt, thinking I'd finish joining the blocks into a top and begin to quilt it. But when I got there with the partly assembled top, the things I didn't like became all too apparent. It was nowhere near finished.

I bought some new fabric, took apart seams, moved blocks closer to their friends, made color modulations that extended further across the quilt, carried brighter colors through to areas that seemed empty, and rejoined seams, only to think of something else I could improve, disassembled and reassembled it some more. It was getting richer, more coherent, more flowing, more colorful, less jagged, less gray. When I returned home, I thought it *must* be resolved, so I joined it into one piece—then excised and replaced a few crucial colors above the center to make them more related to the center colors. Even after the quilt was basted, I switched out a few more blocks to adjust contrast levels. Finally, I began quilting it, changing my mind only a couple of times about the quilting design.

When I had done about two-thirds of the quilting, I realized that what it *really* needed was bright colors around the outermost edge to echo the center. So I unquilted two corners and made 18 new blocks, traded them in, and at last had no impediments to finishing the quilt. (I have a total of 86 leftover blocks. Contrary to my original idea, there are a few duplicate blocks in the quilt.) I had worked on the quilt for about five months. By then it was very close to the deadline—which happened to coincide with another

unprecedented October storm, Hurricane Sandy. I finished the quilt in threatening weather eerily like the storm that had given me the idea for it.

I am notorious in my Round Robin for agonizing and changing my mind, for revising almost-completed quilts, for ripping things that are begging to be finished. Just ask them! This is hardly the first time I've disassembled a quilt top to switch in new blocks or changed my mind about a quilting design. I can't help getting new ideas that are better than my old ideas.

I don't start with a plan, or much of one (though there is a seed, a hope, a color palette that will need to be expanded). I believe a better, more unusual quilt will result without a plan, so it's inevitable that there is uncertainty as the quilt comes into being. The novelist E.L Doctorow said, "Writing is like driving at night in the fog. You can only see as far as your headlights, but you can make the whole trip that way."

This is the eighth time I've been included in NQOF. Eighth! What is it that keeps me coming back for more? I like using traditional blocks; I like linking my quilts to quilting's history. I think it's important for contemporary quilters to understand what so many quilters who went before us loved, and to work with *that*. Because I don't choose the block, I use blocks I wouldn't have realized were as interesting as they are. Any block, really, can be a building block for color inter-relationships—that's the heart of the matter for me.

Until the next emergency, I will be making blocks as colorfully as I can.

Sing Praise

80" x 80"

Photo by Jessica Horton

Meet Ann

Being a country woman living a rural life in north-ern California offers me continual interaction with wildlife, seasonal beauty, and a vast panoramic view of the sky. From the morning's first rays of sunlight over the mountains to sunset's glorious spread of color, our home offers a view of creation that satis-fies my soul and stimulates my creativity. At night, the distant valley lights of our small town sparkle but do not dim the amazing sweep of stars in the sky. Heaven seems to reach out and touch the earth, and I am dazzled by the mystery and majesty of the scene. All of this resonates in my daily life and in my artistic life as well.

Quilting for over 30 years, I enjoy a well-equipped studio with large windows to this view and the gift of time to explore my art and passion to express in some way the joy I feel in this bountiful creation.

Inspiration

This year's block challenge of Jacob's Ladder spoke deeply to me. I have always been fascinated by old names for quilt blocks, and of course, Jacob's Ladder refers to the Old Testament Bible story of Jacob and his dream. I grew up as a farm girl in Illinois and attended a one room country Lutheran school. As a little girl, one of my prized possessions was a little book titled *A Child's Garden of Bible Stories*, which I still have. A picture of Jacob sleeping outside while he dreamed of

a ladder to heaven with angels walking up and down the steps had always intrigued me with the idea of God and his angels being so close to us on earth.

Those dazzling nighttime stars I mentioned ear-lier seem part of this mystery of life so much larger and beyond our scope of understanding. To me, Jacob's Ladder is a moment of connection to God and creation and in that moment, the idea of singing praise flows in me. As a contemporary musician in our church for many years, the phrase "sing praise" occurs over and over in song and prayer.

This would be my Jacob's Ladder: to express in fabric and thread the glory of what I feel every day in this awe-inspiring creation we call home—the beauty of nature reaching out to sing praise to the majesty of our Creator. The beautiful birds would symbolize all of creation and the rich colors and prints of the fab-rics feel earthy and heavenly, all at once.

Almost 20 years ago, I made a doll quilt in the Jacob's Ladder pattern. In this small quilt I wanted to cap-ture the feel of the Civil War era with the fabrics and style.

In my new quilt, I decided to use contemporary fabrics with colors that reflect the greens of leaves; the magenta, purple and turquoise of the sunrise and sunset; soft, misty grey greens and blues of rain and rivers; and the dark colors of the midnight sky. Included in the over one hundred fabrics selected for the quilt were batiks, prints, hand-dyes, and a richly printed deep blue inner border fabric from Italy. Complementing these fabrics would be the beautiful detailed embroideries of birds and butterflies sewn with brilliant rayon threads.

I knew that pulling it all together would be a challenge, but I felt it worthwhile to attempt the hundreds of little triangle pieces to create the surrounding blocks for the embroideries themselves. Searching through my library of old quilt block patterns, I decided on the complex multi-triangle version of Jacob's Ladder because I wanted to design a companion block of a border of triangles for the birds that would mimic leaves in a tree.

The setting evolved as I selected and edited designs for the embroideries that would fit the space. Making a color recipe for each of the Jacob's Ladder blocks, I kept the strong diagonals of the blocks flowing through the main body of the quilt and echoed this in the shaping of the outer borders to create rhythm and balance. I knew that I wanted to pull out all the stops on the embroidered inner borders and this I did: editing, combining, and revamping multiple embroideries to shape them to surround the inner pieced section.

I enjoy adding text to many of my quilts, and in this quilt, I felt the words SING PRAISE needed to be included. A delightful Jacobean alphabet provided colorful and detailed letters to accomplish this task. To balance the letters at the top, I decided to utilize the matching 10 squares at the bottom to showcase butterflies. The two vertical bars of the blue Italian fabric were adorned with threadwork and quilting to highlight the printed fruit and leaves and showcase my collection of WonderFil® specialty threads in various weights.

I used thicker weight rayon threads to outline and quilt the fruits and then very thin 80-weight polyester DecoBob to stipple between the motifs to "pop" them forward. WonderFil® 100-weight InvisiFil™ poly was used in a very light cream color to stipple closely around all of the embroideries and colored triangles to texture the background fabric and let the designs plump forward.

Throughout the quilt, I decided to contrast the very fine quilting of "thin" thread with the ample threadwork of the embroideries and the beauty of the "forward" colored and printed fabrics. Shaping the final outer borders into large pieced triangle shapes was another challenge, but I felt it worthwhile to continue the use of the gorgeous printed cotton triangles and also pull away from a simple square shape and give more diagonal movement to the edges. The final step was to embroider little Jacobean flowers into the triangles on the four corners and then create a fold-over

> *"To me, Jacob's Ladder is a moment of connection to God and creation and in that moment, the idea of singing praise flows in me."*

edge of matching green hand-dyed fabric to give a bit more texture and also complement the Jacobean alphabet in the interior border.

When I design my quilts, I am very conscious of the "repetition with variation" design principle, and keep this in mind with color, shape, and texture in my quilts. The quilt was layered with Pellon® Legacy™ wool batting before it was quilted. The wool handled beautifully to support the embroideries and flatten with fine stipple quilting, giving loft where needed.

It is interesting to see how this quilt looks when laid on my grandmother's vintage Jenny Lind bed: the words read clearly at the pillows' edge and the borders are highlighted surrounding the central field of blocks.

Technique: Shaping Embroidery for Quilts

Digitized embroidery is a delightful addition to threadwork of all kinds on a quilt, and the embroidery on SING PRAISE could definitely be considered the frosting on the cake. Beautiful birds, bees, flowers, berries, and branches are all interwoven into scenes of nature that bring meaning, depth, and richness to the pieced blocks and settings. Viewed as a whole, the embroideries sing the meaning of the quilt as they resonate in rich colors and textures. Complemented by the fine textured quilting that helps them to move forward onto center stage, the threadwork takes the spotlight and holds our attention. So how does one even begin to put this all together?

I have worked with embroidery on quilts for the past 10 years and I can say with certainty that it is a learning curve. While literally millions of designs are available for purchase, the careful selection of motifs and the software to take the selected motif to a new level of creativity within the quilt takes patience and building blocks of understanding on how embroidery works. Technology is amazing, daunting, and enticing all at once. Today's sewing and embroidery machines are at the top of the curve in the industry's ever increasing menu of selections for us to consider.

SING PRAISE was sewn and embroidered with my Husqvarna/Viking® Designer SE™ machine and utilized the Viking 4D™ software system to shape the embroideries. I have recently stepped up to the new Viking

Diamond deLuxe™ machine and the new 5D™ software, which offers even more possibilities for embroidery creativity. Pairing software with your machine is the critical factor. Editing designs and combining ideas to fit different areas of the quilt provides ample opportunity to create beauty and versatility in your art.

When I designed the layout for the quilt I was very specific about where I wanted the embroideries to fit. The size of the pieced blocks and the areas of open field were created to showcase the embroideries. Starting with the blocks in the center of the quilt, I selected nine bird motifs that were very complex designs with 60,000+ stitches in each embroidery. I shaped the designs to fit the space by cutting and pasting various branches and leaves to frame the birds and then I began the stitch out on a large piece of the background fabric.

I embroidered these designs and then removed the stabilizer and carefully cut the background to size before I finished piecing each block with the border triangles to fit the quilt. This allows for careful placement of the finished design in the block itself. In the same manner, I embroidered the alphabet letters on the background fabric as a separate unit that I could then cut and piece into the upper border.

When working with such large stitch count and complex color change embroideries, it certainly takes more understanding than "pushing a button and watching it stitch." Mistakes happen, and often I will use my skill with free-motion embroidery to repair problems in the finished embroidery. The final step of fine quilting around the embroidery is also a delicate dance to settle the heavily textured embroidery into the quilt and hold its shape for stability. Choosing the appropriate weight of thread makes all the difference in very close quilting vs. show off specialty thread work.

I am continuing to explore new ways to include digitized embroidery with free-motion embroidery and specialty stitches and threads. The possibilities for creative application are really endless, and the new technology available is continually challenging us all to experiment and achieve wonderful results. Fearless forward momentum is the best approach to learning new skills, and that will be my "stick-to" motto for my artistic endeavors to come!

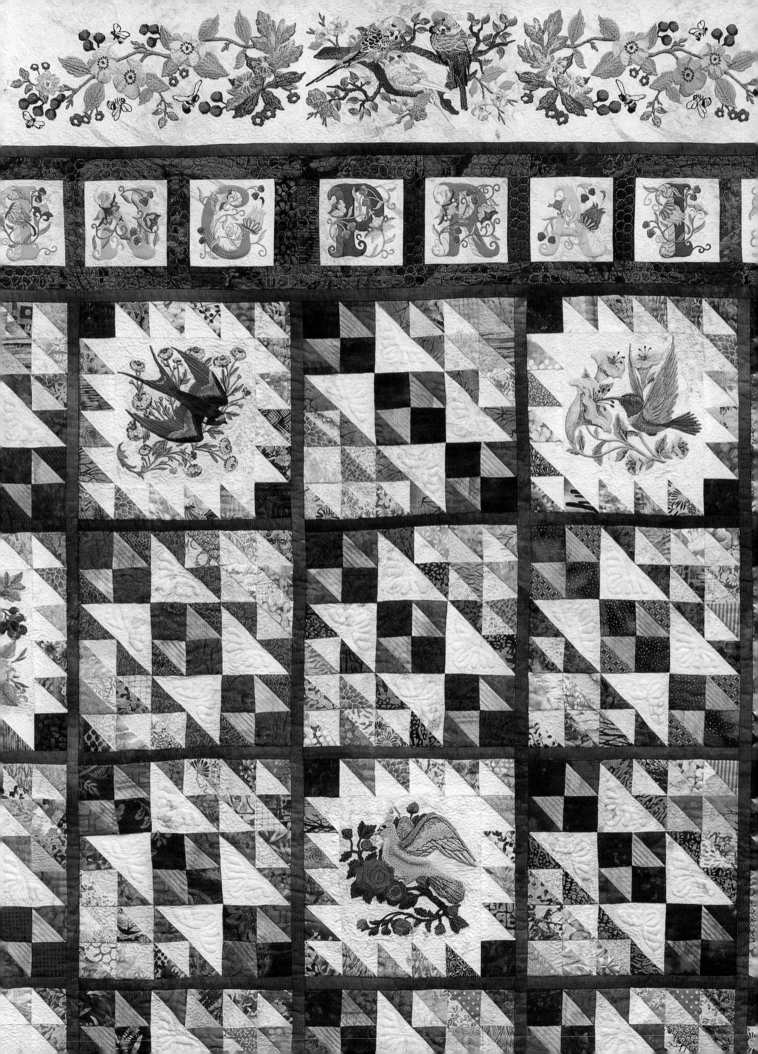

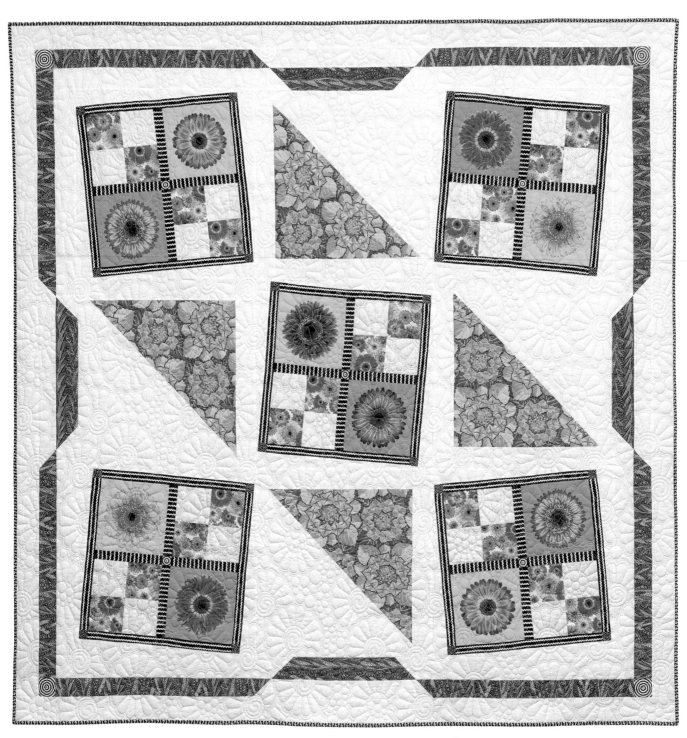

Almost Modern Jacob's Ladder

75" x 75"

Maggie's photo by Hazel DeWitt

Finalists
Maggie Ball &
Wanda Rains
Bainbridge Island, Washington

Wanda's Photo by Everett W. Simila

Meet Maggie

I was born in Northumberland, UK, north of Hadrian's Wall, which technically makes me a Barbarian! We moved to the USA in 1983 and found ourselves in Fayetteville, Arkansas, in 1986. It was there that I discovered quilts. I was thrilled to see them displayed on clotheslines outside farmhouses on the back roads in the Ozarks. After hand piecing 36 Le Moyne Star blocks for my first quilt, I found the local quilt group, Q.U.I.LT., whose members educated and mothered me. They introduced me to the rotary cutter. What a revelation! I loved the endless possibilities as well as the joys of sharing a common interest with other enthusiasts.

We moved to Little Rock where I was active in the Arkansas Quilters' Guild. That group included several exceptionally talented quilters whose innovative approaches to both traditional and contemporary quilting were inspiring and influential. We now reside in the beautiful Pacific Northwest.

I enjoy creating my own designs from elements of traditional patterns and my quilts have been exhibited nationally and overseas. Teaching quilting is a natural extension of my passion and I find it rewarding. When I began quilting as a hobby, I never imagined that it would become a profession and provide me with so many amazing opportunities to travel and share with others. I love teaching and am known for my ability to work with quilters of all skill levels. It is great fun to see what each student brings to class and how they develop what I initiate. I always encourage my students to experiment and audition a variety of options.

One of my favorite facets of quilting is how any pattern can be presented in so many ways simply by the choice of fabrics, placement of different values, and the orientation of block components within the block. Add onto this the numerous ways of arranging and setting the blocks plus borders and the possibilities are endless.

I am the author of four books published by Krause Publications. *Creative Quilting with Kids* and *Patchwork & Quilting with Kids* encourage adults to pass on the quilting tradition to children. *Traditional Quilts with a Twist* contains new patterns derived from the traditional Bear's Paw, Trip Around the World, and Ohio Star. My fourth book, *Bargello Quilts with a Twist*, features quilts made from my original, easy to construct, 16-piece Bargello block. Most recently, I have developed a template-free technique for making traditional Kaleidoscope blocks and have produced a variety of patterns.

As a volunteer in Mongolia in 2004, I taught quilting to low-income and unemployed women. In 2006 I helped organize the First International Quilt Show in Mongolia collaborating with quilters from the UK and Japan. I headed a capital campaign raising $80,000 to purchase a permanent facility for the Mongolian

Quilting Center in Ulaanbaatar. It was thrilling to teach at the new Center in 2009 and my association with Mongolian quilters continues. You may read more at my website, www.DragonflyQuilts.com.

Meet Wanda

I began my quilting journey in 1989 after moving to Bainbridge Island, Washington, from Anchorage, Alaska. In October of that year, I was smitten by quilts in the window of Heirloom Quilts in Poulsbo, Washington. By the time I walked out of the store I was signed up for a beginning quilt class, and had about $100 of fabric in a bag, with no idea what I was going to do with it. As with most quilters, the rest is history. Quilting has shaped my life in ways I could never have imagined. It is my contention that the activity of quilting, and the quilting group itself, fulfills not only our need to create, but an intimacy with others whom we would have never met if it wasn't for this wonderful hobby.

In 1997, after selling my company, I was faced with what to do next in my life. It took much research, soul searching, and a leap of faith to open a longarm business. With my friends' encouragement and support, it took me about two years to perfect the pantograph and gain the courage to move into the custom arena. My technical skills served me well, and over the next 15 years, I managed to earn many awards and entries into the likes of Paducah, Houston, and many publications and books. Maggie and I have been collaborating for all of these 15 years.

After a neck injury and surgery in 2003, I was faced with a decision to close my business or purchase a computerized Gammill® Statler Stitcher® and keep going. Without it I would not be quilting today. It afforded me the opportunity to continue to quilt for my clients while my neck healed, and explore the new world of computerized quilting. The computer does not deter me from freehand work as it is truly the best of both worlds. I still do a combination of freehand custom work and computer-generated designs because I love all aspects of machine quilting. I decided in early 2012 to retire from the professional realm to have more time to pursue my own work. I do rent out my Statler, and spend much of my time quilting with friends and playing tennis.

Inspiration & Design

Maggie

The New Quilts from an Old Favorite concept is right up my alley. I enjoy taking a traditional quilt pattern and interpreting it to produce an imaginative design. The simple geometry of the Jacob's Ladder block appealed to me and I decided early in the year that I would like to make a quilt for the contest.

These days we hear so much about "modern quilts" that I began hatching an idea to design something that emulated the "modern" look. So, what is modern quilting? In an article in the *American Quilter*, Volume XXVIII, No 5, Weeks Ringle describes it thus: "Making quilts that are expressive of the time in which we live rather than re-creating quilts from another century is the motivation for most modern quilters." She goes on to say, "Modern piecing includes an array of styles including improvisationally pieced patchwork, quilt tops constructed from recently designed blocks… as well as those made with non-traditional layouts."

In practical terms, many of the so-called modern quilts use solid colors, large pieces, and expansive areas of negative space. Most do not have borders. They look fresh and contemporary for use in a modern home.

My quilt has some modern attributes—big pieces, sizeable background areas of white, skewed elements for an unconventional layout, and a clean contemporary

"I knew I wanted to enlarge the Jacob's Ladder block but my inspiration didn't really develop until I came across the large flower panels."

look. However, aspects of it are much more traditional and contrived, like the use of prints that are deliberately fussy-cut with precision and the inclusion of a border. Even the white fabric is not solid white, but a white-on-white print, and, of course, the quilt is based on a traditional block. I named it Almost Modern Jacob's Ladder to reflect, in a rather tongue-in-cheek way, this dichotomy. Of course, by definition, it must be modern because I've only just completed it!

I knew I wanted to enlarge the Jacob's Ladder block but my inspiration didn't really develop until I came across the large flower panels. The size of these determined the size of everything else and the quilt grew larger and larger. The choice of fussy-cut fabrics in a variety of scales is what makes this quilt interesting. The design is very simple. Several friends called it a "happy quilt." I like this! When I saw how Wanda had quilted it, I just smiled. The big floral quilting design in pretty variegated thread so perfectly enhances the fun, light-hearted nature of this quilt.

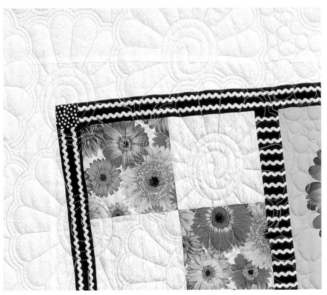

Technique

Maggie

The Jacob's Ladder block is a Nine-Patch composed of five double four-patch units and four half-square triangle units.

I enlarged and separated the units so that they float on the background. The double four-patch units are tilted, giving the quilt a whimsical look. The half-square triangles remain squarely set and of course the white half of the unit merges with the white background making the large print triangles even more distinctive. The quilt is machine pieced.

For the five double four-patches, I cut ten 8½" square big flowers. The small four-patches were strip-pieced from 4½" strips of the zinnia and white with pink fabrics. The lattices and frames were fussy-cut 1½" strips of black-and-white fabric. Note how I changed the direction of wavy stripes. I admit to cheating slightly where the lattice meets the frame. There was a partial white wavy line showing, so I used a Sharpie to black it out! The fussy-cut center squares and the cornerstones on the frames are cut 1½" x 1½". To tilt the units, I added 2½" wide white frames and then trimmed them. In this diagrammatic representation, created in Electric Quilt EQ7 (www.electricquilt.com), the grey area shows the part that was trimmed away. When the remaining piece is set squarely, the unit is skewed on the white background.

I fussy-cut the large print triangles 18" on each of the two short sides and attached 3" wide white strips to the short sides. I added large white triangles to make the units into squares, then trimmed them to exactly the same size as the double four-patch units, then assembled the nine units.

By this time I had run out of white fabric, so purchased another white to complete this quilt that seemed to expand every time I turned around. I fussy-cut the leafy green border fabric, again varying the direction of the print. I planned to stagger the pieces with square ends, but after constructing them and auditioning them with the quilt top, I was dissatisfied and decided to add the white triangles to make the 45-degree transitions. These echo the triangle units in the center of the quilt and make the border more attractive.

The Quilting

Wanda

Maggie's modern design and the large-scale elements on this quilt provided a unique challenge. Sharon Schamber's Daisy Stipple seemed like a perfect fit. We were pleasantly surprised and very pleased with how the longarm pattern and Maggie's vision married together. The pattern included the bubble background fill between the flowers, but by separating the rows slightly, I was able to freehand additional bubbles for increased impact. We used Quilter's Dream wool batting for its beautiful loft and the thread is polyester variegated pastels by Maxi Lock® Serger Thread.

Star Light

64" x 65"

Photo by Robert Crine

Finalist
Deb Crine
Marco Island, Florida

Meet Deb

Up until about ten years ago I didn't know what a quilt was. I'm sure I had seen quilts, but they just didn't register. In 2001 I asked my husband, Bob, for a sewing machine. I had never owned a sewing machine and as far as I knew, no one in my family did any sewing. We had just moved into our home in New Jersey and I thought it would be fun to make pillows and curtains. How hard could it be, right?

Armed with my new $200 sewing machine, I took a ride to Jo-Ann Fabric and Craft Store®. I purchased some fabric to make pillows and spotted a beautiful yellow and blue quilt on the wall. I thought, wouldn't that be pretty with my new pillows! Luckily, it was a quilt kit and even better, since at this point I had never seen or heard of a rotary cutter, the fabric pieces were already cut. All I had to do was sew it together. How hard could it be?

I had no idea what a seam allowance was and didn't bother to find out. I simply put the quilt together, sewing as close to the edges of each piece as possible. I didn't have a quarter-inch foot, and honestly, I don't even think I knew what that meant. When I finished I thought it had to be the most beautiful thing I had ever seen, and I fell in love with quilting. Needless to say the quilt fell apart rather quickly, but that didn't deter me. I found out there was a local quilt shop just a couple miles from my home and began taking every class they offered. I was addicted.

In 2008, my husband and I moved to Marco Island, Florida. Up to this point I had never been a member of a quilt guild. I saw an advertisement for the Naples Quilt Guild and joined right away. I entered two quilts in their annual show. I had never been to a quilt show and asked a few of my friends to come along. When we walked into the show I went on sensory overload. All of those beautiful quilts and vendors to boot! To my surprise I walked away with two first-place ribbons. I didn't stop smiling for days.

As a result of joining the guild, I met three women who would change my quilting life. Pat LaPierre, Suzanne Sanger, and Cheryl Costley met on a weekly basis and asked me to join them. I didn't know them, but I thought it would be nice and probably some fun. Little did I know how talented and giving these women were. They not only taught me everything they knew, they gave me the confidence to try anything. To this day we continue to meet and I look forward to sharing my journey with each of these women for a long time to come.

Quilting totally consumes my life. I am very physically active and began doing triathlons a couple of years ago, but just about everything takes a backseat to my quilting. I usually have at least three quilts going at any given time—one in the design phase, one in the construction phase, and one in the quilting phase. I like being able to jump back and forth among them. I am very lucky to have a husband who is proud of what I do and totally gets why quilting is so important to me. On top of all that, he's a great cook!

Inspiration and Design

Design is probably my favorite part of the process. For each of the past two years I have designed a large quilt using EQ (www.electricquilt.com). I like to think of this as my summer project. We spend a couple months each year at our home in New Jersey and I like to take a project that is ready to be sewn along with me—one that's challenging to construct and will keep me busy for a few months. When I heard about the NQOF contest and saw the Jacob's Ladder block, I thought this would be perfect for my next piece.

I had heard the term *Jacob's Ladder* and knew there was some biblical story, so I began to research that on the Internet. I started thinking about using the blocks to create a background that looked like a ladder and began sketching some ideas, but it just didn't feel right. Too literal and not what I was going for.

One of the things I love to do when designing my quilts is to place traditional blocks into non-traditional settings—sort of like the square block in a round hole theory. The results are often times amazing and it's just simply a lot of fun. I knew I wanted to use at least three of the block variations. I loaded my EQ software and two of the blocks from the block library. The third one had to be drafted, so I got busy doing that.

By this point I knew I wanted a layout that looked like a star. I tried not to think about construction techniques. I've found that if I worry that I won't know how to construct something it stifles the creative process. I hadn't started to think too much about fabric choices, but I wanted this piece to sparkle. Generally I work with very vibrant, what I call "happy" colors. For this piece I decided to challenge myself and use a more subdued palette. I created over 100 variations before I was satisfied that the piece had the look and feel I was trying to achieve.

While I was researching Jacob's Ladder on the Internet, I stumbled across the Jacob's Ladder wildflower. I hadn't

4 trial designs and the final design.

> *"I usually have at least three quilts going at any given time—one in the design phase, one in the construction phase, and one in the quilting phase."*

known it even existed, but I knew that I had to include this beautiful flower somewhere in my quilt. I also knew that with all the spikes and hard edges in my design the flower would provide a nice contrast and help soften the piece. As luck would have it, I found an embroidery design for the wildflower online at the Embroidery Library, Inc. (www.emblibrary.com).

Since I was working with a palette that was very unusual for me, I didn't have much in my stash that was suitable. Several years back I had ordered ten yards of a buttery silk crepe. For the life of me I don't remember why, but it must have been some big project! I decided to use this in white areas. Although it looked beautiful, it would later turn out to be a challenge.

Techniques

The majority of STAR LIGHT is foundation paper-pieced. Although the paper removal is a bit tedious, the results are worth the effort. I've tried many paper foundations and my preference is a product by Deb Karasik called Perfect Paper Piecing Paper (www.debkarasik.com). It's very lightweight, comes in various sizes, holds up well when you are piecing and removes easily. I use a very small stitch, which makes removing the paper much simpler and the stitches don't come apart. I trim and press all my seams before adding the next section.

I decided not to use stabilizer on the silk. I had eight sections coming together in the center of the quilt and I knew this was going to be challenging enough without the extra bulk.

I did a sample embroidery design on an oversized piece of fabric backed with a heavy stabilizer. I made a template and used it to center the design on the diamond block and cut the embroidery to size. It fit perfectly! I used my embroidery software to create a mirror image for four of the flowers.

The quilting process was a lot of fun because there were so many sections where I could use a lot of different quilt designs. Before beginning the decorative quilting I used a lightweight thread and stitched in the ditch around every piece. This was very time consuming, but made the next phase of quilting much more enjoyable.

Finally it was time to block and trim the quilt. I pinned it to my design wall and used my spray bottle to dampen the quilt. As I did this, the silk fabric in the center of the quilt start to stain. I must have neglected to remove some tiny pieces of the paper at the center and once it was wet the ink bled onto the fabric. I was heartbroken. I had spent months working on this. I thought I would cry but I told myself not to panic.

After several tries at removing the stains, I purchased Swarovski® crystals and adhered them to the quilt top. I actually liked the results and added them to other sections of the quilt. If something like this ever happens again, I'll know not to lose all hope!

JL
61½" x 61¾"

Karen (left) and Robin (right)
Photo by Phillip Grover

Meet Robin

I've been quilting for about eight years and design nearly all of my own quilts. In one way, this Jacob's Ladder quilt was very unusual for me. I ordinarily begin with a quilt title and design the quilt to somehow give "life" to that title; Karen and I were still scratching our heads about the title to *this* quilt as we were filling out the entry forms!

In my quilting, I'm usually inspired by the purely visual. I tend to work mostly with solid and hand-dyed fabrics that enable me to play around with color and value to achieve quilts that strike the eye with drama. I am more likely to use improvisational piecing and raw-edge machine appliqué than other techniques and have lately become enamored of miniature quilts.

Karen and I must have met through our membership in Sinnissippi Quilters, our local guild, but I have no recollection of the circumstances. I always attend the afternoon meetings and she always attends the evening ones, so our introduction must have come through some committee work. When we became more acquainted with each other's styles, we helped form an art quilt mini-group in which the five members challenge one another on small projects that explore a theme or motif or technique.

I particularly enjoy New Quilts from an Old Favorite because it challenges me to combine the traditional and the contemporary and try to be true to my quirky self.

It's a great way for me to honor both the past and the future of quilting.

Meet Karen

It's hard to believe that I made my first quilt in 1980 and even harder to believe that was 32 years ago. Now as I near retirement, quilting will be one of the things I look forward to and my mind knows no limits. It doesn't matter what kind of quilt—traditional, historical, contemporary or art—they all hold some level of interest for me.

I *love* challenges and where they take my own creativity. A local group at one of the quilt shops has a challenge that begins with a center block and then each month we get a color and a block to use to incorporate into the next border. After five meetings, we all have unique medallion quilts. We find that we are typically pushed by some aspect of one of the borders and always surprised by the diversity of the outcomes.

Robin and I have known each other for quite a few years; however, we had not really done any quilting projects together. I was excited last year when she suggested that we join forces for the NQOF contest because we do not necessarily do the same kind of quilts. She prefers art quilts and I tend to be more traditional. We thought the combination might make for an interesting design and as we look back now, it was a wonderfully creative year.

Design Process

Karen

Robin and I had our first meeting last September. It was obvious that we both had some initial ideas we wanted to bring to the table and were surprised to find out we were heading in the same direction. Over the next couple of months we spent a lot of time tweaking an idea that we both agreed on. I used my AutoCAD® program at work to sketch, sending out .pdf files for comment and the design seemed to come together quickly. Color did not.

We started with the idea of using a focus fabric for the background and choosing colors from there. Next we picked a group of colors that we thought might work well together but it seemed as though every time we put them together, we were limiting ourselves to a star motif. We were so focused on this process that we xeroxed fabric, made a paper mockup of the wedges and used a mirror to see the result.

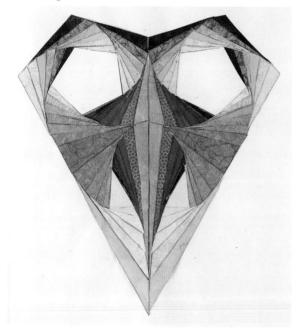

Finally, we decided to try shades of two colors. This worked well and we got a burst of energy that led to several hours at the quilt shop trying to get just the right combinations of reds and greens without the finished product looking too Christmas-y. However, no matter what dark green we put with the other colors, it made it look like a Christmas quilt.

One of the pleasant surprises in quilting is how choices get made. We were just about to leave a joint work session when we noticed a green fabric in one of the containers we had overlooked. It was a Jinny Beyer fabric we had considered and rejected but we had not ever looked at the back of the fabric. We were both amazed when the back side had just the right tone and depth we were looking for. Lesson learned. Thanks, Jinny, for saturating your fabrics with color.

Technique

Foundation paper piecing seemed to be the only way to accomplish the construction. The wonderful thing about paper piecing is that we could both do parts and once it was put into the whole, no one could tell who did what.

As we proceeded through this stage, we encountered a construction issue. How were we to insert the arced pieces into the paper-pieced wedges? Here's how we did it.

Arced pieces: Cut templates of the three parts that make up the arced piece, sew these together. Cut a

"We thought the combination [of our styles] might make for an interesting design and as we look back now, it was a wonderfully creative year."

template using a heat-resistant material and use it to press the seam allowances on the curved edges of the arc. Set this assembly aside.

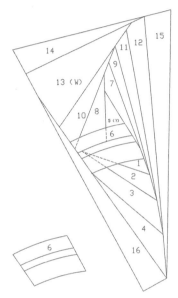

Begin piecing the paper-pieced part using a traditional method. Complete pieces 1 thru 5. These will go behind the arc.

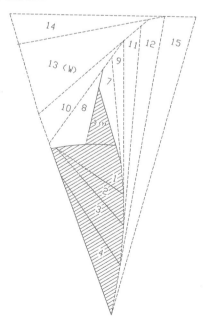

Inserting Arc: Before piecing #7, insert the arc into the seam allowance and sew piece #6 in place.

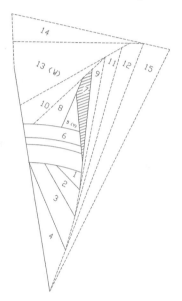

Pin the arced piece out of the way

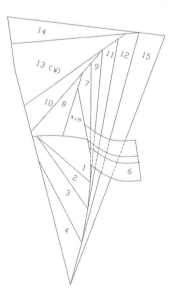

Continue piecing until you complete all but piece #16. Before you sew this piece, lay the arc down so that it will be in the seam. Sew piece #16 into place.

Appliqué the curved edges of the arc in place either by machine or by hand. This will complete the wedge.

Once the wedges for the center section were sewn together, we needed to stitch it down to the backing fabric and design the remainder of the quilt. We worked at this for a while but couldn't settle on effective borders and corners. Back to AutoCad. Several iterations later we settled on the curved border, worked out the patterns for paper piecing and moved on. Unfortunately, we needed to turn the corners. They were the last part of the design to come into play and we did not really design them until we saw how the rest of the quilt looked.

As we approached the point where we needed to start quilting, we tossed around a few ideas, but just couldn't seem to settle on anything. One of the ideas we had was to ignore the quilt and create quilting designs that crossed over colors and seam lines

We both worked on different sections and came up with quilting designs that we both liked. Responsibility for the actual quilting was shared, each of us quilting the sections we had designed. This was perhaps the most stressful part of the entire process. Neither

of us was looking forward to the quilting as we both consider that a weak spot in our quiltmaking. We traded the quilt back and forth several times to finish the quilting, each of us gaining a little more confidence in our abilities.

Quilting done, we thought that the overall look needed to be enhanced just a bit and applied crystals and couched some Razzle Dazzle™ thread around the squares. Both of us felt that gave it just enough sparkle to set it off.

Collaboration

Robin

Just a word about collaboration—the first time is a journey; enjoy it. Here are some of the things we learned about successful collaborative quilting:

Park your ego at the door—this quilt isn't about the singular you but about the collective you. If you can't relinquish total control or if you just can't play nicely together, give it up before your friendship becomes a casualty. While we may not have signed a contract to this effect, Karen and I both well understood what was at stake and vowed to put the friendship first.

Recognize that each of you approaches the quilting process differently. Respect those differences and make them work for you. I think Karen is more deliberate in her designing—she brings the perfect combination of an art degree and a career in engineering to her work. I think I belong to the "throw it up on the wall and see what works" school of quilt design. Each of those approaches played a part in getting to our final design.

Each person brings strengths and opportunities to the collaboration. Be eager to learn from one another as it will result in both of you becoming better quilters. I got to practice my hand appliqué (even though I wanted to the do the appliqué by machine) and

Karen had a good chance to design some complex quilting designs that helped her gain confidence in her machine quilting.

Enjoy the social aspect of collaborative work. It's not all business—share coffee, a bagel, some chocolate. Karen and I scheduled frequent work sessions and we always made sure to include a mini show-and-tell. When we viewed each other's work and engaged in give-and-take critiques, we often got fresh ideas for JL.

Share the work equitably. It doesn't matter how you decide to divide the work as long as each of you feels that it is a fair division. No one wants to feel over- or under-burdened. Early on, Karen and I decided we would each do everything—paper piecing, appliqué, quilting, sandwiching, binding. We didn't just do the things we most enjoyed; as a result, we both developed a healthier respect for the whole process.

Respect one another's time constraints. Work at a pace that allows each of you to fit your contributions into your busy lives. Karen has a full-time job and quilts in the evenings and on weekends. I do a fair amount of community work but my time is more flexible than hers. We established a rough schedule of

when we wanted each part of the project finished and tried to stick with that. We worked around vacations, illnesses, and visits with grandchildren. Be mindful of contest deadlines, too.

Share the expense equitably. While Karen and I did not keep detailed records, we each pulled some stash fabric and purchased thread and fabric as needed. I think it evened itself out but keeping a running tally would have been a good idea.

Be honest and open when offering constructive criticism. If you *really* don't like something, say so; conversely, if you *really* can't live without something, say so. Making changes doesn't mean sacrificing your artistic integrity. Your goal should be to make a quilt that you both feel proud of. It clearly won't be the same quilt you would have made alone but that's not the point.

If, during the process, you recognize that it's just not working out, agree to disagree and abandon the joint project. Maybe one of you wants to take over sole ownership and finish the quilt alone. Please don't lose a friend over the choice of fabric or stitches that aren't perfect.

Climbing Higher

50" x 50"

Photo by Amy J. Graber

Meet Julia

I was born and grew up in the Shenandoah Valley of Virginia and moved to Mississippi after I met and married Paul Graber. We have five boys and one girl and now enjoy six grandchildren. We live on a farm near Brooksville raising grain and hogs and are also involved in a small trucking company. We are members of Magnolia Mennonite Church and enjoy the fellowship and activities of our local brotherhood as well as mission activities in Romania.

I learned to sew when I was young and made a few quilts soon after we were married and as the children were growing up. It wasn't until after our youngest went to school, that the "quilting bug" really bit me. My sister Polly suggested that I subscribe to *Quilters Newsletter* for a starter. I did and it opened my eyes to the quilting world out there. That was back in 1996. I soon subscribed to other quilt magazines and started making more and more quilts.

When Nancy Ryan asked me to share my quilting journey with the Mississippi Quilter's Association, I felt very unsure of myself. However, I was willing to share the story of my gradual introduction into the quilting sphere.

Then when the Possum Town Quilters formed a guild in 2004, I joined as a charter member. They have provided me with lots of inspiration, encouragement, challenges, and contests. I'm also a member of AQS, NQA, and MQA.

My first quilts were mostly utility type, bed-size quilts. I still like the traditional and scrappy large quilts but recently I'm drawn to smaller sizes and art type quilts. I've heard that it's good to work in a series, so I've tried making smaller teaching type quilts, Volcano/Mountains, Abstract—What Mean These Stones, a Pines series, and photo challenge quilts.

I have enjoyed teaching workshops, giving trunk shows, and Power Point Presentations at different quilt venues. You may visit my blog, Life as a Quilter—Julia Graber (http://juliagraber.blogspot.com) to learn more about my life and how I just don't have enough time to sew and quilt.

Inspiration, Design, and Technique

I am challenged in taking an old familiar quilt block and turning it into something new and innovative. The New Quilts from an Old Favorite contest provides just the challenge for me to do that.

I enjoy using EQ7 (www.electricquilt.com) to start the process and pick out the traditional block pattern and set it in different layouts. I set four Jacob's Ladder blocks together (left), then rotated them like this for my layout (right).

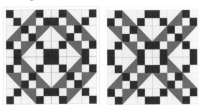

From there I set a Twisted Log Cabin block into some of the squares of the Jacob's Ladder blocks.

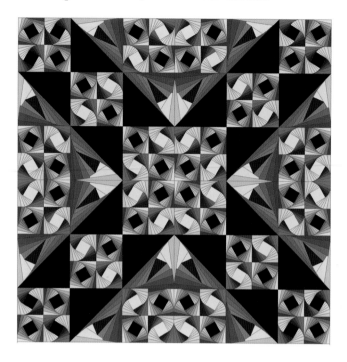

This made the quilt way too busy, so I designed and drew a triangular Twisted Log Cabin block that could be set into the triangles of my layout.

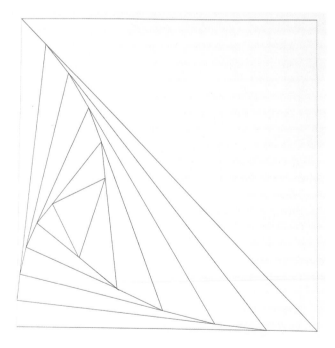

From there I rotated and flipped the blocks and tried different color schemes.

"I still like the traditional and scrappy large quilts but recently I'm drawn to smaller sizes and art type quilts"

I printed out the blocks for foundation paper piecing, then sewed, and joined the blocks. I incorporated the center "rung" element into a border.

I was right pleased with my quilt and began quilting in the center. But alas, my quilting did nothing to improve the quilt top. It bubbled and puckered quite awful! I had used two layers of batting hoping to achieve a grand trapunto look. Not so! So, what to do? I cut all the blocks apart as close to the stitching seam as I could. This gave me smaller blocks, but I was OK with that.

I laid out the blocks again in different arrangements, settling on the final arrangement. I quilted each of the blocks separately, then sewed the quilted blocks together with a quilt-as-you-go technique, which allowed me to quilt smaller units with my home sewing machine with better precision and a walking foot. I used the same fabric as the center element of the "rung" blocks for the sashing to coordinate with the border.

After binding the quilt, I blocked it by placing a vinyl tablecloth on the carpet. I laid the quilt on top and squared it up placing pins 3"–4" apart around the perimeter of the quilt into the carpet through the vinyl. Then I poured about a gallon of water on the quilt and patted it down to get all the fibers wet. I sopped up any extra water with a towel. Next I turned a fan on and blew air over the quilt and let it dry overnight.

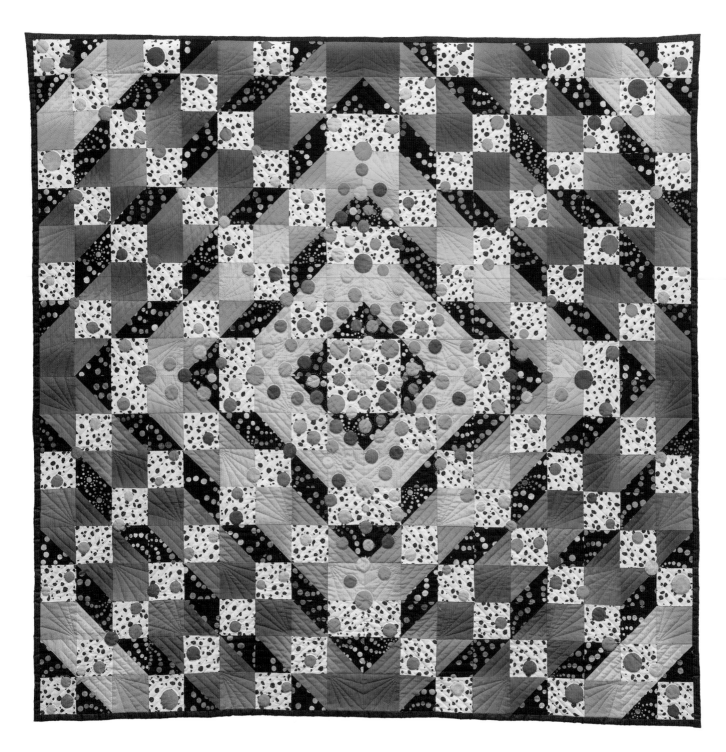

Pathways
73" x 73"

Photo by Jack C. Herndon, Jr.

Meet Mary Ann

I was probably always destined to become a quilt-maker, but like most other travelers I took some detours along the way. Those detours or experiences of sewing clothing, doing needlepoint, painting, etc., all contributed to finding a craft that I have enjoyed for years. Probably the turning point for me was a lecture by Yvonne Porcella at my first Houston Quilt Guild meeting. Her originality and use of explosive color led me to trade in all my other "hobbies" and focus on quilting. Like most quilters at the time, I started with patterns and instructions, but through the years I've progressed to creating my own original pieces and preparing a lot of my own fabrics.

I constantly find inspiration from the work of others in the quilt world as well as artists in other media like painting, book illustration, and commercial advertising. Lately, two painters, Mark Gould and Todd Schulten, have influenced the choice of color and design in my work. Creating a quilt to me is no different than creating a painting. It is disturbing that some quilt critics don't have the background to appreciate the vast history and evolution of quilts as an art form and still refer to them as utilitarian bed covers that their grandmothers made.

I retired 12 years ago from my job as the library director for a local suburban school district. We had lived in the same house for over 30 years, and, in the last 12 years we have built two wonderful homes with art studios for me and have just moved into a high-rise condo that we have spent the last year and a half

Finalist
Mary Ann Herndon
Houston, Texas

gutting totally and remodeling. I digress to tell you about this because I think my quilting evolution has a parallel to my choices in home design.

Our taste in decoration started with the very traditional and our newest home can be described as transitional but not contemporary. It has a fairly neutral background punctuated with color by the wall art and "texturized" with all the finishes we selected. The quartzite in the kitchen covers most surfaces and soars to the ceiling. Each inch of it is a feast for the eyes.

We switched from our previous dark alder doors and paneling to a dusty taupe. The large display blocks covering one wall in the study are perfect for the natural colored Hayes Parker sculptures we've collected. My husband's desk is topped with a leather finish granite and the design that sweeps across it would inspire any contemporary quilter.

Several of the large paintings we have bought through the years would inspire most quilters. Marcia Meyer is one of the artists who layers paint to create massive blocks of intensive color. If I ever machine quilt, I would like to take her ideas and do something with machine quilting. The paperweights and kaleidoscopes I have collected are great sources of design and color inspiration. I have incorporated houses in some of my work and their inclusion has been somewhat influenced by my collection of Mary Fisher stone houses. In the hallway leading to the bedrooms, I gave up a much needed closet and inserted 24" inch cubicles to display large pieces of glass. I could go on telling you about all the visual stimulation available to me in just our condo, but, I will finish by mentioning the glass and stone in the bar, the lighted onyx in the powder room, and the quartz trim in a bath.

What I am trying to emphasize is that an environment that includes all sorts of art, whether it's great finishes in the walls or collections you love, is a plus for stimulating inspiration and creativity. If you can't create such a place from scratch, take a look at all the interior design books and magazines where there are endless ideas for color and design. Mixing different textures and patterns in interior design as well as in quilts creates interesting palettes.

Technique

To develop a design for PATHWAYS, I first chose a version of the Jacob's Ladder block and revised it by changing the diagonal blocks into solid ones rather than the traditional four-square ones.

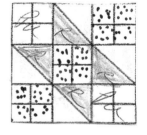

Then I shaded in some components to make a black-and-white pattern, made many copies in a small size on a copier, then, spent some time arranging the blocks until I found a design that appealed to me. The final arrangement allowed me to use the shaded fabric I had chosen to great advantage in the squares that move out from the center.

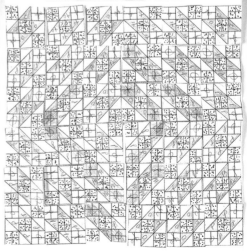

> *"An environment that includes all sorts of art, whether it's great finishes in the walls or collections you love, is a plus for stimulating inspiration and creativity."*

The quilting was dictated by the components and the shading in the blocks. The appliquéd circles were added after the quilt was pieced. It seemed to need some additional surface aspect to emphasize the center and the pathways leading to the center; circles were a compatible choice since two of the fabrics had dots and circles.

Before I started cutting block components, I labeled my mockup with the fabric colors so that the shading progressed from the center to the outside edges. The blocks in the quilt are 12" square with 4" components.

I find a design wall is invaluable in my work. When we remodeled the condo we're in now, we designed one of the bedrooms to be an art studio. The design wall takes up one wall. I saw this idea by Carol Taylor in a magazine article about her studio and when I contacted her about some details my contractor had to know before he built something similar for me, she graciously provided me with the information I needed. My builder built shelves across the whole wall for fabric storage and then installed three 8' x 8' homosote-topped sliding doors in front of the shelving. I have easy access to my fabric since the doors slide and the surface of the doors allows pins to be used in planning quilt designs.

Inspiration and Design

I have entered this contest before and been fortunate enough to be included in the finalist group several times. The idea of changing a traditional pattern so that it retains some recognizable aspects of its original form but allows a new interpretation is a challenge I have found intriguing. Color is always my starting point while design is the second consideration. A good design depends on many ingredients, but the proper use, placement, and selection of color is paramount.

Bearing this in mind, a shaded vibrant gradated fabric already in my stash was an easy choice. It allowed me to arrange colors that radiated from a central point. The block arrangement was chosen so that the design also radiated out from a central point. I especially like the shading in the blocks that the gradated fabric made so easy to do. A fabric that shades into different colors results in a much different progression of color than using separate colors to achieve a progression. This design can be easily modified through color choices to make this an original for most any quilter.

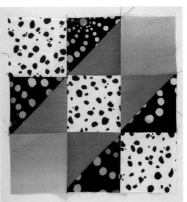

Capra hircus
73" x 73"

Photo by John K. Hobbs

Meet Pat

When I was very young, growing up in Kansas, I wanted to be a "cowgirl." My step-grandfather bought me my first cowgirl boots. I participated in small bore rifle competitions on an all-girl team at the Topeka, Kansas Police Department during my high school years. That is as close to becoming a cowgirl as I came. By age five, I thought I might grow up to be an artist. In junior high, I researched and wrote an essay about fashion design. I had been making my own clothes from age 10. My mother reasoned with me that I could have one store bought dress or two homemade dresses for the same price.

My research revealed that most fashion designers began their careers sewing in a dress factory. That didn't appeal to me. By high school, I was leaning toward interior decoration. Mrs. Cook was my wonderful home economics teacher in junior high and high school. My father stepped in and suggested that if I was going into the fine arts, maybe I should be a teacher. That is where my career began, and I taught visual art in public schools and colleges for 34 years. I made extra money by restoring and dressing antique dolls and selling my paintings.

It has only been in my retirement years that I have zeroed in on fiber art—quilting. Prior to this, most of the quilts I made were for baby gifts. Now that I had a little more time to work on the things I chose to do, I made art quilts and began entering them into quilt show competitions. I had done the same with my artwork, so I knew it was more enjoyable to share my

quilts in the same manner. My husband purchased a new sewing machine for me, a BERNINA® 440 QE, making the quilting process much more enjoyable. I do like making pictorial quilts and trying the new methods of working as they come along. I am also at the age where family history has become interesting so some of my quilts are genealogical in theme. My last genealogy quilt, NEW ECHOTA, was done to honor my husband and his Cherokee (Tsalagi) ancestors. This quilt was entered into The National Cherokee Holiday Quilt Show that is in honor of the signing of their constitution on September 6, 1839. It won a blue ribbon in its category and succeeded in making my husband very proud.

NEW ECHOTA

My son was featured on a wall quilt, WILL @ FIVE, that was in the 2011 AQS Quilt Show & Contest in Paducah.

WILL @ FIVE

Inspiration and Design

I love challenges like New Quilts from an Old Favorite because they make me think outside of my comfort zone. In the case of Jacob's Ladder, it would mean that more piecing than I usually do would have to be done. I keep a list of quilt ideas that I would like to make, and sometimes I have collected the fabrics that would be used on a listed quilt. My challenge was to look at the list and see what idea could possibly be adapted to work with the Jacob's Ladder theme. This was a dangerous method of working as it might box one into a single thought or idea that does not allow the brain to see creatively; other possible ideas and solutions might be better, but are not allowed to be envisioned.

The concept for this quilt came from a piece of Helene Davis's hand-dyed fabric (www.hand-dye. com). I envisioned a quilt of purple fabrics, cold and wintery. The main figure was to be an Ice Queen. I must have been depressed when thinking this color scheme would be interesting. A complementary ombre of sunset colors in aqua blue and orange was substituted for the darker colors. When purchasing new fabrics, I found the orange and the blue-gray with purple print materials. Both of these fabrics had printed curving, spiraling, vine-like designs that fit right in with the overall quilt design. These fabrics became part of the "golden mean" theory, which is to repeat the design in various proportional, decreasing sizes. The scrolls were the repeated image found also on the maiden's dress and hair and in the vines on the Jacob's Ladder trellis.

I had lace pieces that would be perfect for the icicles or hanging flowers. The scroll designs on the dress were inspired by the artist Gustav Klimt. The maiden's hair was an adaptation of work by the artist Alphonse Maria Mucha.

I enjoy the designing process the most. This is probably why I have such a long list of quilt ideas to be made in the future.

Technique

The full-size pattern was drawn on news-print paper using the 8½" x 11" sketch for reference. Color notations were written on the pattern. The pattern was cut apart and used to either pin to fabric or trace around with a marking pencil.

The first step was to piece together the sunset background that fell within the rectangular trellis. The

> *"I enjoy the designing process the most. This is probably why I have such a long list of quilt ideas to be made in the future."*

bands of color would then be carried to the sides of the quilt and flow through the Jacob's Ladder pattern. This trellis was to frame the ice queen and two albino deer. A photo of these deer was first seen on the Internet. Unfortunately, I was unable to receive permission to use the image. Consequently, the deer were replaced with a couple of white domestic goats (*Capra hircus*). The goats were drawn while my *Plein Air* (fresh air) painters were visiting the Western Illinois University farm that has these goats. (We are a group of women who go outside once a week to draw or watercolor scenery.) The four squares of the Jacob's Ladder pattern would remain constant with the two vertical squares in white and the horizontal squares in purple.

Next, the dark purple sumac tree silhouettes were machine appliquéd onto the center panel. Following that, the blue-gray scrolls were machine appliquéd over the Jacob's Ladder lattice using a blanket stitch. The lace appliqués were intertwined with the scrolls and hand sewn onto the quilt top. These would be encrusted with beads after the quilting was completed.

I had made a face for the female figure and planned to add more curly hair using thread play. However, this face seemed too pale and petite for the setting of the dark purple trees. I decided to return to my original three-quarter turned face and make her hair into tangled scrolling curls that would be machine appliquéd onto the quilt.

I am aware that some quilters think the face should be pieced rather than drawn with oil pastels. Coming from a fine arts background, I prefer the softer blending of colors to the hard edges of piecing. Drawing and painting on canvas is the same process as drawing and painting on cotton or any other fabric. The oil pastels should be allowed to dry for a few days and then heat set-with an iron to become permanent.

The female figure was appliquéd by sections: hair, the flower wreath, face and neck, hands, dress, and then the shoes. Helene's hand-dyed fabric had distinct veins of the dark purple. While the fabric was beautiful all by itself, in this quilt it seemed too light. I drew designs that fit within the veining. These pieces were fused and then satin-stitched to the dress with hand beading to be added later.

The goats were drawn on tissue paper to scale, cut out, and both raw-edge and hand needle-turned appliqué were used to put them on the quilt. They too were drawn with fabric marker and oil pastels. I knew that the quilting on the goats would represent their fur. It was interesting to note that the live goats

had the same kind of a tracking chip in their ears that is used in quilts, allowing the goats' progress to be monitored from all aspects: amount of food eaten, weight gained, sale price, etc.

The main problem that I encountered with the appliqués is that I used a heavy fusible webbing. The glue would gather on the machine needle, clog the eye, and fill the groove on the needle's front side. Although one of Laura Wasilowski's commandments from the Chicago School of Fusing is, "Do not kill the glue on the fusible web," I was trying to do just that by holding the iron on just a little longer. I thought if I "killed" some extra glue, it might be easier to quilt through. But quilting the large scroll vines and purple trees was too difficult, so I used a blanket stitch around the edges. Fortunately, they were stiff enough to hold their shape without the quilting.

In summary, the Ice Queen turned into a goat maiden, the color scheme became brighter, and the Jacob's Ladder trellis remained the same as depicted on my original drawing.

Jacob's Ladder Infinity
59" x 59"

Photo by Yu-Hui Kuan

Meet Lin

I am an independent artist devoted in creating quilt art. My recent works have been recognized by exhibitions held both domestically and internationally. I am also one of the core executors of a local quilting society in my hometown of Tainan, Taiwan. We have regular meetings and participate in social welfare activities from time to time.

I teach quilting courses at the National Tainan Living Art Center. I really enjoy teaching. There was an old saying that teaching and learning mutually support one another. I sometimes feel that it is me who learns the most from my students. I manage my own quilting blog (http://tw.myblog.yahoo.com/playquilt-goodtime) and join various art groups in order to share my joy as a quilter.

I used to be a full-time housewife. Quilting and my world merged in the year when my younger son was still in kindergarten. It started as simply my pastime, but gradually climaxed as I devoted more and more time in this art. During the eight years since, my dedication to this art form has strengthened my belief that the spiritual satisfaction and wealth nurtured by interest is definitely positively correlated with better quality of life.

For me, the apparently ordinary and repetitive hand-sewing job in making a hand-crafted quilt is not only a skill training of patience and perseverance, but also an essential procedure of transformation and subli-

mation beyond pure skills. The basic steps in making a hand-crafted quilt intensifies my feelings about the meaning and spirit delivered from this art—if it is handmade, it should be unique; if it is unique, it should be touching, the touching moments from daily life—to embrace life passionately, to feel life full-heartedly, and to quilt devotedly. This is a circle that turns my inner communication mechanism on, as well as embarks a self-searching journey through time. In the end, I learned to reevaluate and re-ensure my own existence.

As one of the chairpersons of the Taiwan Quilt Art Society, I was honored to help hold international quilt exhibitions twice (2009 and 2012) in Tainan. Artists from 22 countries contributed more than 200 quilts. I had opportunities to meet with these artists in person. They were indeed precious experiences. I am hoping that maybe someday, I can be the one being invited to share my experiences overseas.

Creating quilts, participating in an art society, and teaching quilting are all emphasized beside my family life. Quilting is not just quilting to me anymore.

Inspiration and Design

Where can we find the zest of life? I think it is in fact from details in our daily routines. My quilt art is expressed in both concrete and abstract fashion, sometimes even a mixture of the two styles. The theme in my creation surrounds environmental issues mostly. I sincerely hope that via this gentle,

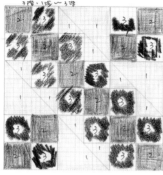

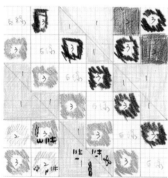

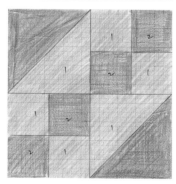

artistic power, the art may be able to become a wakeup call for human beings to respect mother earth.

Creating in the form of a quilt is pleasant for me. I really enjoy every step in the procedure. Sometimes the processes exhaust me to a point where I think I will no longer have the energy to continue with creating. Nevertheless, I always find myself regaining my power to come back with even more joy.

Just to come up with original design ideas takes a lot of time and energy. More challenges are yet to come as I consider how to divide the whole into interconnected parts, how to transform colors to fabric blocks, how to enforce or even create new figures through special quilting design, how to add other materials properly in order to enrich the design, and how to complete border design so that the story completes beautifully (or at times how deliberately not to end the story so that the trace of it can linger in the air).

My training background in quiltmaking was almost all in hand-sewing tradition. However, when I heard about this contest, I decided to challenge myself with a new task, which was machine sewing without using templates. Preparation beforehand had to be precise and exact, which included a miniature full-scene overview, color blocks in each single area, scales and quantities of each cut-off unit. I deliberately chose the scales of lines and the colors of patterned fabrics to pop out of the frame of the background.

Technique

I used a rotary cutter to cut all the fabric pieces, then joined the pieces from the smaller ones to the relatively larger ones. Therefore, pre-production preparation was essential.

First, I hand-drew a miniature design for the whole quilt.

Second, the detailed design of each unit was drawn and colored.

Having finished all the detailed plans, I calculated exactly how many pieces of each fabric would be used and rotary cut them all at once. The precise working procedure might seem to be complicated at first glance, but I can assure you that it will save you at least half of your time spent on material preparation.

"The basic steps in making a hand-crafted quilt intensifies my feelings about the meaning and spirit delivered from this art"

Next, I tried the "assembly line" technique, through which the same kind of steps would be completed at once by machine-sewing.

And then, all the semi-final assembled blocks were sewn together according to the original draft. I followed a schedule every day as much as possible so I could finish the quilt in time as I had planned.

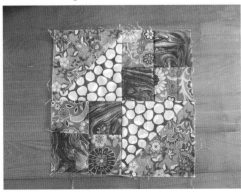

In sum, most of my techniques are traditional ones, such as traditional piecing/appliqué, reverse piecing/reverse appliqué, thread sketching, and embellishment. Binding the quilt is the technique I feel most proud of! Too bad it is impossible to demonstrate in words or static pictures. I sincerely wish one day we can meet face-to-face so that I'll be able to share that with you, my dear quilting circle of friends.

Substance of Things Hoped For
53" x 67"

Photo by Emily Smith

Meet Amy

I live in the Baltimore area with my husband (married twenty years and still counting) and two children. I work part-time as a software engineer. And I quilt. Oddly, my husband seems perpetually surprised by this. "Didn't you just finish a quilt?" he keeps asking. "Don't you want to take a break?"

It started twelve years ago when my sister was about to have a baby. I wanted to give her something special. A quilt was born ... oh yes, and a nephew as well. I had made him a small Log Cabin quilt, chain-pieced in a weekend, and I was addicted.

I had done a lot of sewing before that, mostly garments, some of which even fit me. But quilting was different. It was more creative, and it didn't have to fit anyone. And I could buy all those pretty cotton fabrics that would have ended up permanently in the ironing basket if I had made clothing out of them. At the time, I was a stay-at-home mom with a two-year old son and a five-year old daughter. It was good to have something to think about besides Thomas the Train and the feigned consumption of plastic hamburgers.

I checked out almost every quilting book in the Baltimore County library system, and looked forward to watching Alex Anderson's quilting show whenever it was on. I learned about the existence of freezer paper, and sure enough, there it was in my grocery store. Who knew? I began experimenting with different techniques while making quilts for friends and family and various rooms of our house.

I went to the state fair that year and looked at the quilts on exhibit with the eyes of a new quilter. Those quilts were awesome. They were amazing. The next year I went, they were still amazing, but I thought to myself, "I could do that." And I did. I was thrilled when I won a third place ribbon for my entry.

A few years ago, I saw the pictures of the winners of the NQOF contest and again I thought to myself, "I could do that." I decided to enter in the Orange Peel contest. I spent eight or nine months on it, finished it in the nick of time, and entered. I was crushed when I got the e-mail saying it did not get in. But in late December, my husband got a phone call while I was out: a quilt had been disqualified because it did not meet the size restrictions. My quilt was in. Picture me doing the happy dance.

That got me motivated to enter the next contest, NQOF: Baskets. I spent 10 months on an elaborate design that included the Basket block transformed into trees, land, and water; intricate piecing, and raw-edge appliqué of four related scenes using unusual fabrics from different countries; foundation pieced borders; fabric paint and markers; and the best quilting I had ever done. No one could reject this quilt ... except NQOF.

So, I searched the Internet for other shows in which I could enter that quilt—the Mid-Atlantic Quilt Festival (in), NQA in Ohio (Judge's Recognition ribbon), and the Maryland State Fair (Grand Champion!). So, thank you, NQOF, for challenging me to do my best work.

Inspiration and Design

I did not intend to make the Jacob's Ladder quilt, but I couldn't resist playing around with the block in my Electric Quilt (www.electricquilt.com) program. I came up with a nifty star design out of skewed blocks with an asymmetrical zigzagging border. It looked so simple, but it appealed to me, and it fit with the theme that was beginning to develop in my mind. It was much easier than the basket quilt; it wouldn't take long to make. I would just throw it together and move on to other things (by things, I mean quilts, of course).

As I thought about the quilt, the name of the block brought to mind the Bible story of Jacob. He has a dream in which he sees a stairway to heaven with angels ascending and descending on it. In the dream, God promises that He will be with him and make him a blessing to all people. The angels moving back and forth between heaven and earth implied to me that God is actively involved on this globe of ours. God's promise to Jacob suggests that He will provide what we need to fulfill our purpose in becoming a blessing to those around us.

I wanted to make a quilt that represented my faith that God has a plan and a place for us even when it is not easy to see. I named it SUBSTANCE OF THINGS HOPED FOR after Hebrews 11:1—"Faith is the substance of things hoped for, the evidence of things not seen." To illustrate the idea of things hoped for becoming substantial, I left a block of plain fabric on which I quilted the Jacob's Ladder pattern, so that the design progresses from being done just in thread to being pieced in fabrics.

I chose quilting designs to emphasize the theme. I quilted angel wings climbing up and down the zigzagging border. I quilted flowering plants (which I based on Jacob's Ladder plants), illustrating the growth from the roots (what is not seen) to the leaves (signs of progress) to the flowers (now we are getting somewhere), and finally to fantasy flowers (something that we don't even yet think is possible). The grapevine alludes to the Christian metaphor: being connected to God enables you to live a fruitful life. The city in the top right corner is my visualization of a place of peace and community. The blue ribbon in the top left corner: well, a girl can hope, can't she?

So, I threw that quilt together in a jiffy—it only took 10 months to complete, and nobody needs to know that I was quilting every spare moment of the last month in order to finish it in time.

Techniques

I began the quilt by foundation paper-piecing the star segments. I recently learned a technique on some quilting show (I wish I could remember which one and who was teaching it) that uses freezer paper and does not require actually sewing on the paper. There are several reasons this method is an improvement over actually sewing the fabric to the foundation. First, you do not have to tear off the paper when you are done. It will just peel off in one piece so you can re-use your paper pattern. Also, you can iron each seam open or in either direction. And the best thing about this technique is that it is easy to ensure that your next piece of fabric is aligned correctly and big enough to cover the next area on the pattern.

To use this technique, you draw your pattern reversed on the non-shiny side of the freezer paper. The woman who was teaching the technique recommended that you sew without thread along all of the lines of the pattern to perforate it so that it folds easier. I do not bother with that step. It is a little harder to fold, but manageable.

"[Quilting allowed me to] buy all those pretty cotton fabrics that would have ended up permanently in the ironing basket if I had made clothing out of them."

Iron the first piece of fabric to the shiny side of the paper, making sure you have at least a ¼" seam allowance of fabric around the pattern piece.

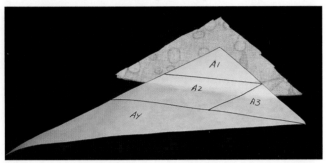

Fold the freezer paper non-shiny sides together along the pattern line where you want to add the next piece. Lay out the next fabric right side up. Place your work in progress with the fabric right side down on top of your next fabric. Line up the freezer paper fold so that you have about a ¼" seam allowance above it, and the freezer paper for the next area is entirely on top of the next fabric (with a seam allowance around it). For example, in the picture below, the area outlined in red is entirely on top of the blue fabric.

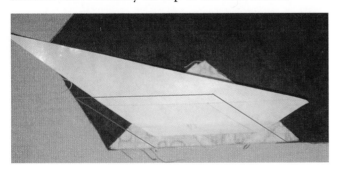

Sew right next to the folded edge of the freezer paper, being careful not to stitch on the paper.

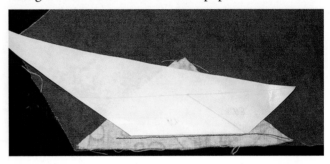

Open out the freezer paper and iron it to the second fabric. If you want to change the direction of the seam or open it, you can peel back the freezer paper a little and do so.

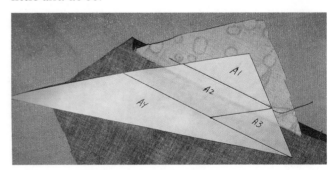

Trim a seam allowance around the second piece of fabric. Then fold the freezer paper again to add the next piece. That's all there is to it.

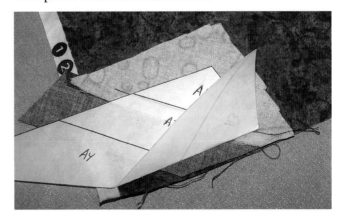

JL Tribute
55" x 55"

Photo by Nancy Lambert

Finalist
Nancy Lambert
Pittsburgh, Pennsylvania

Meet Nancy

I have been quilting for well over 20 years and continue to have more and more ideas about designs and quilts I'd like to make.

At any one time I will be working on several quilts. I work on both traditional and non-traditional quilts. Some are made for a bed and others are art quilts for the wall. I am now involved in a monthly appliqué class where I am learning new hand-appliqué techniques. I try to take classes and learn new techniques as much as possible. I have met so many wonderful friends over the years by being involved in quilting.

I have worked on many aspects of quilting from dyeing my own fabric to designing patterns. I enjoy both working on traditional patterns, but also creating new designs.

Inspiration and Design

I enjoy working on design and interpreting a new idea in a different way. My design aesthetics continue to evolve. Using scale has become one of my fundamental design tools. Starting with the simple square and triangle shapes that are in the Jacob's Ladder block provided inspiration for this quilt.

I took both the square and triangle shapes and created many variations. For the square, I tried breaking it into smaller squares and had sample blocks that had the square broken into 4, 9, or 16 individual pieces.

I also tried making concentric squares with the basic square and then a smaller concentric square or two progressively smaller squares. I used a similar technique for the triangle shape. I broke one triangular shape into three smaller triangular shapes. There are also concentric triangular shapes used.

These variations resulted in dozens of blocks that were auditioned in many different combinations. These combinations were pinned up on the design wall and viewed from a distance. Blocks were tested with other blocks until the overall scale felt appropriate.

Once the scale and combination of blocks were in place, color was introduced. Mostly solid colors were used. The hard line between different colors, where there is no pattern, created strong visual impact. Warm colors or cool colors were used for most shapes. For instance, each triangle that was broken into smaller triangles would either have warm or cool colors. If warm colors were used then three different warm colors that complement each other were used. These color variations help give visual interest and keep your eye moving.

With all the bright solids, some black and white fabrics were added to provide resting areas. These areas were added once most of the rest of the design was done.

Satin stitching around many of the blocks adds another dimension to the quilt. The wide satin stitch, which was up to ¼" wide, frames the individual pieces. From a distance you may not notice the satin stitching, but as you get closer you see the color and depth.

The final border around the overall quilt is made up of satin-stitched squares on a white background. Each of the squares is the same size. As you see the border these outside squares appear to be a little larger or smaller and not all the same size. The color of the satin-stitched thread gives them the illusion of different sizes. Some of the squares appear to be receding back and others protruding out. This adds a modern feel just by the use of colors that advance or recede.

Technique

This is a technique that can be used with any basic shape. Let's start with a triangular shape.

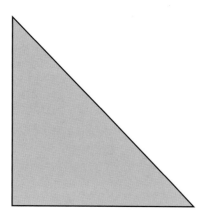

This is a right triangle, meaning that it is formed by a square with a diagonal drawn between the opposite two corners. Break the triangle interior into three smaller triangles by drawing three lines from a point in the center to the three corners.

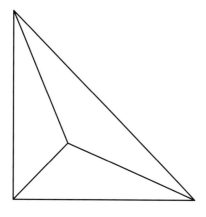

You can play around with the sizes of the smaller triangles and adjust them to get a pleasing size. These smaller triangles are about the same size. You could also have two of the three smaller triangles being larger. Different sizes will give a unique feeling to the block.

Once you have broken the shape into smaller sections, you can work with various colors to create the feeling you are going for. Here warm colors are used with the block. These could be any color and fabric combination you find pleasing.

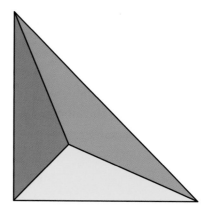

You could take this idea one step further and break up each of the three sections in the same way that the original shape was divided. In this variation, cooler colors are used.

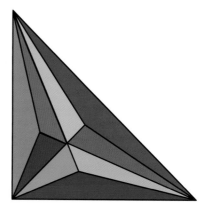

This block could be pieced or fused depending on the look you are going for. Solid colors are shown, but patterns and prints would also produce great designs.

"Using scale has become one of my fundamental design tools."

Lady Bug Ascent
72" x 74"

Photo by Cynthia A. Briggs

Meet Tina

"Grandma, I just don't have time to quilt now." That was a statement I made close to 20 years ago. My grandmother, who lived less than a mile away, had been ~~bugging~~ encouraging me to start quilting. From the time I was young I had loved to sew. My mother says that at first I learned how to make drawstring bags; all she required is that I ask before cutting into a piece of fabric. She says that I had a bag for everything I owned.

As I got older I began making my own clothes, including my own "designer" jeans. I played with the stitches available on the machine we had. My mom was great encouragement in those younger years, pushing me to learn more and do it better. I hated having to rip something out, but she would say, "If it isn't right, you won't wear it." Therefore, she would help by picking out the stitches and I would redo it properly.

At nine years old, my aunt gave me a quilt that she had started from fabric that was left over from family members' clothing; it is a parasol doll pattern. Mom stitched it to a white background, then I spent many hours embroidering arms and edge stitching the entire design. Then it went into hiding.

After I got married, I acquired a Singer® that made curtains, clothing, and, yes, my first quilt. I used a cardboard template, cut up scrap fabric into six-inch squares, used a blanket to fill it, and tied it with embroidery floss. I was so pleased with that first quilt, but didn't make another quilt for many years later.

Then I was working full time and keeping up with two busy children. I was making all of their clothes, coats, and curtains for the new old house. "I don't have time to quilt." Yet my grandmother continued to ask and, with persistence, I finally agreed to make a sampler quilt. She coached me through the process, showing me the new gadgets that she had discovered, including a rotary cutter, ruler, and cutting mat. This was the true beginning of my journey into quilting.

One of the things that Grandma had discovered was a walking foot that would allow you to quilt in the ditch on your home sewing machine. I was intrigued by this because I had pulled out that parasol doll quilt every once in a while; I would hoop it up and stitch for a week or two until I got sick of pricking my fingers, and then, away it would go again. So I purchased a walking foot. Then I saw on a television show that with another foot, I could move the quilt around freely and quilt that way also. I went to a local quilt shop and took my first class on free-motion quilting; I remember I had to put metal washers under the footplate on my machine because I didn't have drop feed dogs. And the rest, as they say, is history. I made and quilted a few quilts on that old Singer; I was so impressed with myself for being good at "that thing" they called stipple; you know, where you could not cross two lines.

In 2006 I began working in a doctor's office with Cindy Briggs, a nurse who was a prolific machine quilter. At the time I was making quilts from the traditional patterns; I was the traditional one and Cindy was the artsy one. We became fast friends and have been close ever since.

In the winter months, my home becomes a busy Saturday retreat for friends who want to learn. They see my success as well as my failures, and I hope they learn that if you try, eventually you will succeed.

I still work full time, but the time I spend sewing/quilting every morning before I go to my job is my therapy; it gets me through those busy, sometimes exhausting days at work. I always look forward to finishing those unfinished projects and beginning new projects.

Once in a while I still pull that parasol doll quilt out, and yes, it has been almost 40 years since I stitched those first black lines in it. It now has binding and is almost done. Someday I will smile when I put that last stitch in it, but for now I continue to call it my 40-year quilt. Maybe by the time I am 50 I will consider it done or not. When I am in the quilting zone, or out at a show I often think, "If Grandma could only see me now."

Inspiration and Design

In the spring of 2009, Cindy and I took our first trip to Paducah. Early in the morning we climbed onto a bus, loaded with eager quilters, and the adventure began. What a wonderful time we all had. I had never seen so many wonderful quilts, or so much beautiful fabric. That is the year I purchased the fish fabric for LADY BUG ASCENT. We were at the fairgrounds and it jumped right into my hands. This beautiful fish fabric, which I used for the half-square triangles, is where my design began. I also purchased the coordinating striped fish fabric, but as you can see, never used it because the quilt didn't like it.

I begin with graph paper and the original block design. After playing around with the design, I dis-

covered that the purple star was showing up as a secondary design, and if I lined up the rows I was able to add the green spinning stars.

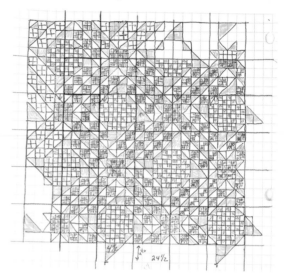

It took a few tries, but eventually the spin showed up on the star, and I was able to make the sections work together. I chose fabric from my stash inventory and colored the design accordingly. For me, using "peeper papers" helps to keep my design straight as I am putting sections together; I'm able to keep everything going in the right direction.

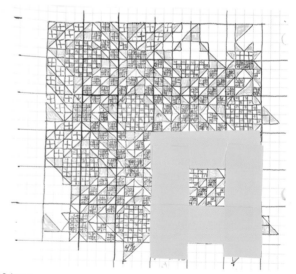

Using peeper papers

The title came from red and black fabrics that made the four-patch units look like lady bugs. The border was necessary to keep the spinning under control and

> "The title came from red and black fabrics that
> made the four-patch units look like lady bugs."

give the quilt an ending and the backing fabric is a hand-dyed piece of white-on-white.

I laid the backing on my floor and taped it down, then added batting and the top. All layers were spray-basted lightly and then pinned together. Yes, I pin the layers also. It makes me feel safe. Then I start quilting. Here is where the real lessons begin.

Lesson 1: In the past I have basted the borders of a large quilt with my walking foot, using dissolvable thread; this keeps the top layer from migrating to areas where I don't want it. After many days of quilting, the thread did NOT dissolve. Always try a new product out exactly the way you plan to use it. My fingers still hurt from picking that out of my quilt.

Lesson 2: If your quilt speaks to you, listen. I decided to quilt feathers in the borders; the quilt was telling me not to do it. After quilting an entire side with feathers, the quilt was screaming to me, "NOOOO FEATHERS." Yes, I picked stitches for over a day because of that, too.

Jacob's Winding Ladders
72" x 74"

Photo by Thilo Schüller

Finalist
Birgit Schüeller
Riegelsberg, Germany

Meet Birgit

Coming from a family with lots of creative talents—my mother is a seamstress and my father a dentist with lots of craftsy skills—and having been into knitting and having tried almost any other craft there is, I discovered piecing patchwork and quilting by accident in 2001, when my almost four-year old son had caught chicken pox and I was banned from the office!

I taught myself the do's and don'ts of quilting from books and magazines and immediately started quilting on my domestic sewing machine. From the very beginning, I have tried to come up with my own twist to familiar patterns and, as early as February 2002, I was asked to teach classes at a friend's quilt store.

Since these humble beginnings, I have come a long way. I have been operating my successful longarm quilting business in Germany, Creative BiTS (www. creativebits.biz/en), with an international customer base since 2005. Over the last six years, I have won numerous awards in major European and international shows. I design, piece, and quilt all of my show quilts and garments myself. My piecing designs are based on traditional patchwork but I challenge myself to take these traditional roots to contemporary levels.

My studio is my hiding place and my comfort zone. Quilting is my fulfillment, my creative outlet, my therapy in all walks of life, and, yes, it also is a source of income for me and my family. I'm self-employed—and sometimes that's the worst aspect; the only person to blame for any task that needs to be done or any project that has been accepted is me, myself, and I! But I love it this way and wouldn't want to have it any differently!

Inspiration, Design, and Technique

Confronted with a theme for a quilting challenge, I either have a pretty clear-cut idea about what I want to do right away, or I most likely never will. When I read about Jacob's Ladder being the 2013 theme for The National Quilt Museum's New Quilts from an Old Favorite contest, I first of all looked up the exact wording of the story in the Old Testament. I then knew immediately that I wanted to find a way to express that the original biblical story of the ladder to enlightenment still has a very strong significance in our times and in modern life. I was all excited!

I learned about this contest in November 2011, about 10 months before the deadline, which definitely was far too early to seriously get to work on this project right away. But I began to toy around with my idea.

In order to achieve my vision of a star with wonky lines extending from and/or leading to a bright center, I knew some manipulating had to be done on the computer. I drew a basic Jacob's Ladder block in Corel-DRAW® (www.corel.com) and stretched it in a way that turned the square block into a 60-degree diamond. Using different distortion tools, I turned the straight lines into curved ones, testing which bends I liked best.

When I was satisfied with the result, I printed my diamond master template to size and from this I traced six identical diamonds on the thinnest embroidery stabilizer I could find.

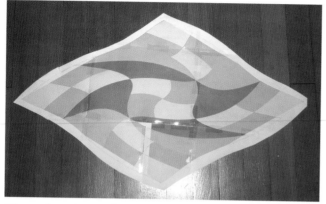

Diamond master template

Then I was stuck.

Next, the holidays came and went, followed by quilt show entry deadlines and other projects, and all of a sudden, my generous 10 months had dissolved into thin air and all that was left before the contest deadline were a few short weeks! This turned out to be my greatest challenge with this project – TIME, or the lack thereof!

I decided to back out of this challenge, but after I had shared this decision on Facebook, two dear quilting friends of mine stepped up. Kimberly Einmo, whom I had shown my draft to half a year ago, insisted that I simply *HAD* to make a quilt from this design and the other, Leona Harden, pointed out that this project needed neither to be a full-size quilt nor to be pieced! These two statements tickled my ambition so that I got to work right away. Thank you, my dear friends, Kimberly and Leona!

So, on a Friday night exactly two weeks before I had to ship the finished quilt (!), instead of working on the customer quilts piling up high in my studio, I pulled out dozens of batik fabrics from my stash to find the ones that spoke to me. Although I had never been a convinced fan of raw-edge fusible appliqué, I jumped in with both feet and had a blast! What fun it was to cut out the exact size patches, to peel off the paper from

the fusible webbing on the back, to arrange the patches on the foundation according to the outlined pattern and to fuse everything in place one patch at a time! I felt as if I was assembling a mosaic. It was a quite different way to "piece" a quilt top; plus it was incredibly FAST!

Assembled diamond

I sincerely am planning to include more fusible appliqué in my work in future projects as this adds quite a bit of spontaneity and surprise to the process.

When the six curvy diamonds that form the star were assembled, I had three choices about how to position them—with all the light yellow tips forming the center (below left), with all the dark golden tips forming the center (below center), or the alternating version (below right).

Choices.....

choices....

choices!

"Time turned out to be my greatest challenge with this project."

After some more playing, contemplating, discussing between me, myself, and I, I chose the third option since this setting added the most movement to the piece. The "ladder" bands marking the long axis of the individual diamonds now seemed to alternately extend from and lead toward the center of the star.

With just the six diamonds in place, I thought that there was too strong a focus on the "star" aspect. What could I do?

I turned to my master diamond template again and while laying it out onto the assembled top, I discovered that rotated by 60 degrees, it would fit exactly in between the outer portions of two pieced diamonds! What would have been more logical than to decide to add an uneven edge to the quilt, as this is something that I regularly do in my show quilts? In order to achieve this effect, I traced along the outer edge of the master template and—voilà!

With the master template in place, I also realized that thanks to fusible appliqué I could "extract" certain patches from my design and add them to the otherwise plain background sections with the help of more raw-edge appliqué. Thus, I prepared and cut out six more sets of "ladder" band patches, then arranged and fused them in alternating color gradations around the center star.

Creating the "halo" effect

As an effect of connecting the outer tips of two neighboring star diamonds with a "ladder" band, the star seems to have a halo. At the same time, all of the ladder sequences or bands are connected. This not only softens the geometry of the design a bit, but more importantly it expresses my intention of showing that the original meaning of the biblical Jacob's Ladder story still has relevance today: The roads we are traveling are all surrounding the center—the origin and utmost destination. As long as we are aware of this center within ourselves, we will be getting there—no matter how windy the roads may be!

The cutting, fusing, and assembly process of this quilt top was completed about 48 hours later on Sunday evening! When I loaded my quilt sandwich onto my machine the following Monday, I felt the strong urge to secure the edges of the fused patches but still wanted to play around with quilted and non-quilted areas which I love to do!

Recently, I had treated myself to a six-spool collection of variegated YLI silk thread and this was the perfect project to use them on—all of them! I opted to do some very dense quilting along the edges of the individual patches to avoid any fraying issues in the future complemented by various whimsical quilting designs that change from color to color.

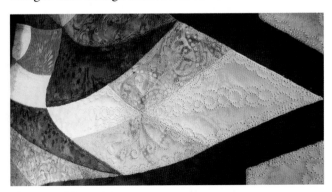

Close-up of the quilting

I always make sure to include quilting designs that are suitable to accommodate hotfix Swarovski crystal embellishment later on. That's one of the reasons that you very often find pebble and various style swirl quilting designs in my quilts.

Star center

To complement the wild and dense quilting of the star patches (which was completed on Thursday evening), I opted to stay a bit more formal and subdued in the background quilting so I chose to quilt semi-whimsical feathers bearing in mind that the outer edge of the quilt would be curvy and irregular. I picked a spool of YLI metallic thread from my thread stash noticing that it was a *SPOOL* and not a *CONE* but not paying any attention to the yardage. I'm sure you can guess what happened. After less than half of the background quilting, I ran out of thread on a Friday evening with no local store carrying this type of thread and no chance to put in a rush order anywhere—remember, I'm located in Germany! I had to have the quilt finished by Wednesday evening of the

next week because of the impending deadline. After several hours of angst, I realized that there was just one thing to do—RIP! And I ripped... Friday night, Saturday morning and afternoon, Sunday morning and afternoon, and finished the job on Monday morning! After days of ripping, I completed the background quilting using a thread that I triple-checked that I had enough of on hand and it only took me three or four hours!

I took the quilt off the frame on Monday evening and used my master diamond template to cut the curvy outer edge. The double-fold bias binding was attached by machine and hand-stitched to the back that night and the following morning.

When all the sewing was done, I took out my collection of Swarovski crystals and another of my favorite toys—the "magic" crystal applicator wand! I always try to distribute the right number of crystals evenly over a quilt top so that the viewer gets the impression of randomness, although each and every rhinestone has been positioned with a purpose. Despite the *VERY* tight time frame, I had fun with the "crystallization" process.

For blocking, I took over my dear son's bedroom on Wednesday—which luckily was one of the days that he is at school all day—and booked my husband for that same night for the final photography session. QUILT DONE!

I still cannot believe it, but I made this quilt from scratch within two weeks, which I never thought would be at all possible! A huge thank you to everybody who followed the process, let me rant, and who offered support during this time. Looking back, the making of this quilt actually is a good example of what I'd like this piece to express: The roads may be windy and unforeseeable things may occur, but as long as we don't lose our perspective and focus on what's important, we can achieve anything—even if it seems impossible along the road."

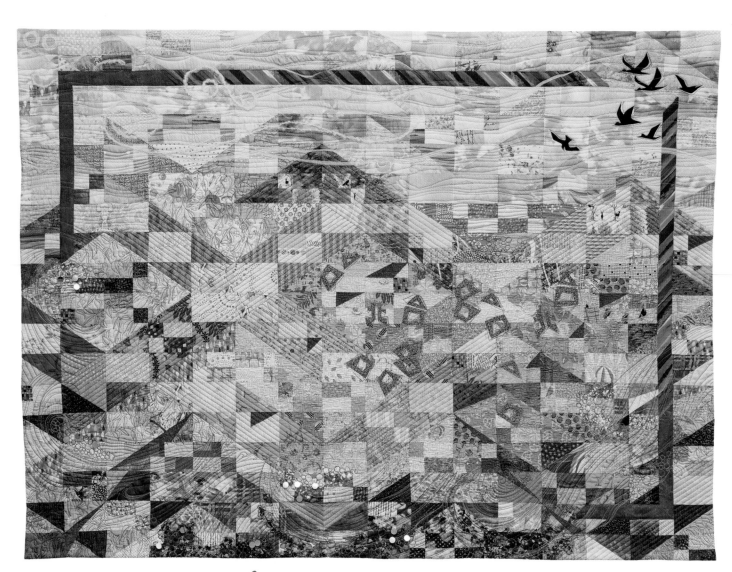

The Taipei City
72½" x 54¼"

Photo by Wang Yao-Tung

Finalist
Tsui-Hua Chen
Taipei, Taiwan

Meet Chen

I bought my first computer sewing machine in 2005. The general merchandise store provided free classes and I took advantage of the opportunity to learn how to quilt.

I continued to attend class unceasingly and to read a lot, for the purpose of promoting my self-ability, and eventually attained Japanese hand-sewing instructor qualifications. In the spring of 2010, I was invited to participate in the Taiwan International Quilt Exhibition. In order to participate, I started to create my own work.

That year I won the best outstanding prize, and it encouraged me to move bravely and diligently forward to create more work.

My architectural design work background also provides a foundation on which I create. I seek themes centered on life and the environment, and these different domains provide me with rich inspiration.

Being a finalist in this contest strengthens my resolve to create my own designs. I now think that traveling the road of quilt art, I can strive to make more works using more multidimensional materials.

Inspiration and Design

I love this wall quilt; this sentiment comes from how I love Taipei City, where I live. I think each artist is convinced that where they live is the very best place for them to be inspired to create.

Inspiration for THE TAIPEI CITY came from one 1932 map. Although it has provided me with an entire wall quilt scene, I was not limited to it or by it.

In the design organization, I took Jacob's Ladder as the main foundation and used a mirror to duplicate and/or stretch changes in the monotonous design. The color choices I made refer to the original map, but finally I added my own ideas and adjusted the entire wall quilt.

Color pencils are my most important tool.

In the quilt, the blue color part is the river; the brown part is the town; the green part is the mountain; and the area above the flesh color, sky blue, and the white is the sky. There are many red scraps in the quilt, which I intended to show the transportation routes of the city. I appliquéd many triangle and square blocks in the town area to give it significance, including the Chinese characters for "Taipei." I am glad to display the Chinese word for my beloved city in this wall quilt.

The quilting of the green mountain part is straight-line; in other parts I utilized free-motion with patterns I developed myself. In the sky, I used lines with lighter colors and simple curves. In the river part, all the lines are curved; sometimes they change to circles.

I like to utilize different materials to make my work with rich expression. In the river part, besides the cotton fabric and the netting material, I stitched tiny pieces of tissue behind netting to represent foam. I also used sequins and free-motion quilting to increase the current of the water. I strengthened the wind-in-the-sky aspect by flowing white gauze in one direction, simultaneously forming the clouds using wool to make the picture livelier.

When I worked, I put the pieces on my bed, which was the only place in my home large enough.

When I was working on this quilt I thought deeply about the inner border as a frame, hoping it would not limit or constrain the dynamic scene. In order to increase the intensity, I finally appliquéd the border as an incomplete, or open frame. This helps the birds break through, enabling communication between the outside world and the town.

The quilting is the second layer of the entire work, with the colors and different threads and materials allowing me to create more emotional expressions.

I seek themes centered on life and the environment, different domains that work to provide me with rich inspiration.

Jacob's Star
52½" x 52½"

Photo by Harvey L. Ziel

Finalist
Susan E. Ziel
Ocala, Florida

Meet Susan

I started quilting in the early 1990s when I discovered that golf only takes a half day. Retirement means filling your time with things you love to do. I had loved fabrics and sewing since age 10. An ad in the newspaper offering beginning hand-quilting lessons at the local quilt shop changed my life forever. I've been quilting up a storm ever since.

I took the beginning, intermediate, and advanced series of classes and have had several other classes at various shops and quilt shows. Quilting is a large part of my life. Like most quilters, I never get bored. There is always another quilt to be made.

Inspiration comes from everywhere. Just open your eyes. I make time to quilt both for charity and family and personal needs as well as for competition. I am so fortunate to live in the sunny south where I can play golf year round and my wonderful husband does the cooking so I can make quilts!

Inspiration and Design

My good quilting friend gave me some antique Jacob's Ladder blocks purchased in a shop years ago. This was my first experience with this particular block. When I saw Jacob's Ladder was the 2013 block for The New Quilts from an Old Favorite contest, I decided to give it a try.

That old phrase "What if?" was the starting point for the design of this quilt based on the old favorite Jacob's Ladder block. What if some of the straight lines were replaced with curved lines? Then what if one of the block sections was a miniature of the whole block? Then what if four large blocks were rotated so that four mini blocks became the center of the quilt?

Using EQ7 software (www.electricquilt.com), I drew the new block and auditioned many color combinations. My practical nature dictated that the final color choice had to be compatible with the colors in my home.

Jacob's Star

Overall Size: 55.00 by 55.00 inches

Quilt "Jacob's Star" in EQ7 Project "Jacob's Star" printed from EQ7!

One challenge for me was to use only three fabrics in this quilt—generally I like to get as many fabrics as possible (up to hundreds!) into a quilt. I really like the bold graphic design of this quilt resulting from so few fabrics.

Technique

Quilt blocks and layout were drawn with EQ7 software. The quilt is made with batik fabrics plus black iron-on bias tape and black binding. This was my first time using iron-on tape and I used four rolls of it. I made plastic templates for each pattern piece and cut out fabric pieces with no seam allowances. Each 9" square block was constructed separately using iron-on bias tape hand stitched along both edges to hold the pieces in place. Then all the blocks were basted onto a muslin foundation on which was drawn a 9" grid.

Long vertical and horizontal bias tape lines were positioned, ironed on, and hand-stitched in place along both edges. Then I layered the muslin backing, Hobb's wool batting (first time using this, too), and the quilt top, and hand basted through all layers.

I drew quilting designs and made plastic templates and marked each block just before quilting. I used the water removable purple marker. I hand-quilted using Sulky 12-wt. variegated cotton quilting thread in the tan and rust fabrics and Mettler® cotton quilting thread in the purple fabric.

The quilt label was also made using EQ7 software with the design printed onto fabric and stitched to the quilt back.

Jacob's Star

by

Susan E. Ziel
5638 NW 27th Place
Ocala, FL 34482

"I started quilting in the early 1990s when I discovered that golf only takes a half day."

The National Quilt Museum

The National Quilt Museum is the world's largest and most prestigious museum devoted to quilts and fiber art. Established in 1991, the Museum aims to advance the art of quilting by bringing quilt and fiber art to new and expanding audiences around the world. In an average year, the Museum's in-facility and traveling exhibits are viewed by over 110,000 quilters and art enthusiasts from all 50 states and over 40 countries worldwide.

Located in a 27,000 square foot facility in historic downtown Paducah, Kentucky, the Museum's three galleries feature exhibits of the finest quilt and fiber art in the world. The Museum's vibrant and breathtaking exhibits are rotated 8–10 times per year. The primary gallery, with over 7,000 square feet of exhibit space, features quilts from the Museum's permanent collection that includes over 320 works of art. The two secondary galleries feature touring exhibits of unique and diverse quilts and fiber art. The Museum also has a number of touring exhibits that travel to museums and quilt shows throughout the year.

The Museum is reputed for its educational programs. Throughout the year, we host educational programs on a diverse number of topics for quilters of all skill sets. Quilters come from all over the

Visitor in gallery

Student in workshop

is truly an exhilarating place to learn more about quilts, quiltmaking, and quilters.

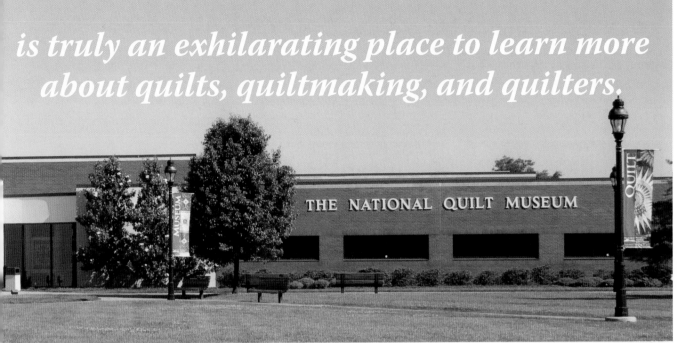

Photo by Charles R. Lynch

world to attend our educational programs taught by master quilters.

The Museum's youth education programs are attended by over 4,000 young people of all ages. Several of these programs have received national media attention. The School Block Challenge, sponsored by Moda Fabrics, is an annual contest in which participants are challenged to make a quilt block out of a packet of three fabrics. Now in its seventeenth year, this challenge continues to be utilized by schools and community organizations as part of their art curriculum in over 20 states. Other popular youth programs include the annual

Gift shop manager Pamela Hill and volunteer Loyce Lovvo

Quilt Camp for Kids, Kidz Day in the Arts, and the Junior Quilters and Textile Artists Club.

If you are reading these words, you are most likely one of over 21 million quilters from the United States and around the world. The National Quilt Museum is committed to supporting your work and advancing the art of quilting so that everyone worldwide can experience and appreciate this extraordinary art form.

For more information about The National Quilt Museum visit our website at www.NationalQuilt-Museum.org.

Instructor Judy Schwender with student

More AQS Books

This is only a small selection of the books available from the American Quilter's Society. AQS books are known worldwide for timely topics, clear writing, beautiful color photos, and accurate illustrations and patterns. The following books are available from your local bookseller, quilt shop, or public library.

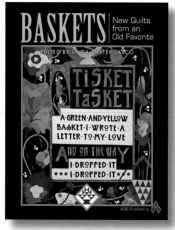

#8669

#8152

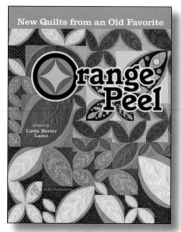

#8350

#1245

#8347

#1246

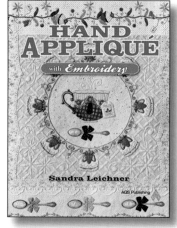

#8244

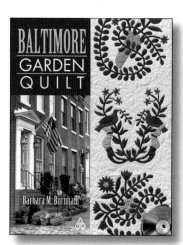

#8672

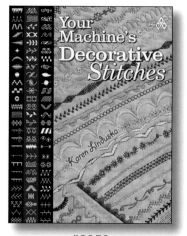

#8353